LIFE
IN
SEGMENTS

ISBN: 9781973566175

ACKNOWLEDGEMENTS & DEDICATION

I would like to acknowledge that God alone has had His hand in the writing of this book. About four years ago my friend, Linda, simply said that I should write my testimony. She said it was not her idea but God's. After this, at a prayer meeting, God spoke and said I should start my story. I must confess that it was a daunting task and at first I was overwhelmed. How would I be able to do this? Finally I came to a place where I simply said I was willing to write it but only if He provided someone to type it. Literally the next day my friend Sylvia said she would type it and that it would not be a problem.

So I started the assignment given to me.

The next year our church had an Easter conference. One of the speakers, Brian Schwartz, prayed for me knowing nothing about me whatsoever. What did he pray?

"Girl, get your story out there!"

This is my story and I am being obedient to get it out there!

I would also like to acknowledge all the support and help I have received from wonderful family and friends

COMMENDATIONS

The Oxford Dictionary definition of ordinary is "... of no special quality or interest; commonplace; unexceptional:" yet when you read 'Life in Segments' by Mary McFarlane you will notice there is really something both unique and special about being ordinary!

To my knowledge Mary holds no official title of any kind or position of office yet as you get to know her through the pages of this book, revealing her life story (so far), it is obvious that though there is no title there is a testimony. Mary is truly an ordinary lass. Just like the rest of us, ordinarily special and unique.

I first met Mary when she turned up at some meetings we were holding in Stirling. This was the beginning of a season of working together in Stirling. There is a common saying in Australia 'A Quiet Achiever' describing someone who doesn't make a fuss or draw attention to themselves but just gets on with it. They do what needs to be done! Mary is a Quiet Achiever.

My wife Kerry and I got to know her quite well through working together. We saw her heart for the Lord and for people, to serve but not to be served. I was particularly intrigued by how she had a 'whole life' approach to people being concerned with all aspects of their lives, not just the spiritual.

Many of us would be familiar with the saying we are not extraordinary people, just people who serve an extraordinary God. Another way to say it is that when we are just ourselves then God can be Himself through us and extraordinary things take place.

Life in Segments is exactly that. From her conversion till now we read the story of an ordinary Scottish woman just being herself and yielding to the transforming power of the eternal life we have in Jesus Christ. Mary's story is one of trusting God in everything and obeying His voice no matter the cost or how it may appear to others. I remember the day when I announced to the church that May McFarlane was now Mary McFarlane, and that is who she was born to be.

God's great love for Mary is all the way through this wee book. A recent song by Jesus Culture says it so well.

"Higher than the mountains that I face
Stronger than the power of the grave
Constant through the trial and the change
One thing remains, one thing remains
Your love never fails, it never gives up
It never runs out on me
Your love never fails, it never gives up
It never runs out on me
Your love never fails, it never gives up
It never runs out on me
Because on and on and on and on it goes

For it overwhelms and satisfies my soul
And I never, ever, have to be afraid
One thing remains, one thing remains
In death, in life, I'm confident and
covered by the power of Your great love
My debt is paid, there's nothing that can
separate my heart from Your great love." [1]

Enjoy this book by all means but let it inspire you to believe that your ordinary life can be uniquely special too. May our lives, with many segments, be like an orange, a sweet fruit to others like Mary is to so many.

Pastor Ron Edwards, Stirling, UK
Church Planting Co-ordinator for Scottish Assemblies' of God

I have known Mary as a friend and fellow minister for many years and can say that she is a woman who hears from God but more importantly is obedient to His voice. Anyone reading this book, wherever they are in their faith walk, will be encouraged to seek more of God. She is an ordinary woman who allows an extraordinary God to work through her.

Barbara Smith
Abigail Ministries Kilsyth

I have known Mary for many years, and have no hesitation in endorsing her ministry. She is encouraging, bold, and displays God's strength in all she does, but at the same time has a huge heart of compassion for those in need of God's touch on their lives. She is an anointed teacher and preacher, opening up the Word of God in a way that is easily understandable. She also testifies to its power in her own life, as she lives what she teaches. Because of this, she is a very popular speaker at ladies events and has ministered widely in Aglow International groups all over Scotland, bringing the truth of God's Word which heals, restores and sets free. Her ministry has seen many released into receiving the Baptism of the Holy Spirit with the evidence of speaking in tongues, the power of which she testifies to in her own life.

Helen Hunter
Aglow International

We are privileged to have Mary as part of our church family. She is a godly lady of faith and has had many experiences with God. Mary is very gifted and has been used greatly as she is led by Holy Spirit.

However, what has impressed us most is her humble, godly character. She has a great servant heart, always prepared to quietly help others and encourage everyone to look to her beloved Jesus.

This book is the story of a real life account of someone who has abandoned their life to Jesus and follows Him unconditionally. Mary is the kind of person God is looking for in these end times and her story will be an encouragement to many.

We thank God for bringing her into our lives and for being able to call her a friend.

Tom and Jennifer Paton

Elim Pastors Paisley

All Scripture quotations are from THE HOLY BIBLE, NEW KING JAMES VERSION, Copyright © 1982 by Thomas Nelson, Inc.

CONTENTS

Newarthill

I was 28 when I celebrated my second birthday. I was born again on July 9th 1982. I vividly remember the journey to Troon where I met Jesus and experienced my second birth. It took me 28 years before I found 'The Way, The Truth and the Life'.

I was born on September 6th 1954 into a good family. The 'Dows' were well known in the small Lanarkshire village of Newarthill. My father was known as 'Mr Chippy.' He had six mobile fish and chips vans that travelled all around the local area. As children, my older brother and two younger sisters and

I, all played a part in the family business. From a young age, my sisters were five and eight and I was nine, we would sit at night making up cardboard fish and chip boxes. Piles, thousands high, kept the vans stocked up for their Thursday to Sunday runs.

Wednesdays were 'filleting fish' days. The smell of fish and the messiness of their scales used to turn my stomach. My younger sister, however, would grab their heads with her hand on their hideous eyes, slide the sharp knife down their side and spine and before you knew it, it was filleted perfectly.

I, on the other hand, after school would steel myself to run into what was called 'the chip house' holding my nose because the smell of fish was awful, quickly ask for the house key before I ran out of breath, and make it back to safety and fresh air outside.

Thursday was the start of making the chips. They started off as sacks of potatoes which had to be put into the peeler to rub the skin off, then they had to be eyed, every last one done individually by hand, before they were put through the chipper and into the bins. Twenty two stainless steel bins full of chips covered in water were done daily every weekend for years.

When I was twelve I was allowed to go as Mr Chippy's serving assistant. We sold fish, chips, black pudding, chicken, hamburgers, haggis, onions, pickled eggs, bottles of ginger (fizzy drinks) and cigarettes. Talk about a great experience. In those days it was all mental arithmetic as we had no calculators. A fish supper was 2/6d in old money. A bottle of ginger was 9d. As well as cooking and serving, my dad kept an eye on my counting and his profits. It was fun and the characters we met each week were diverse to say the least! People also came to the house at all times of the day or night for ginger or cigarettes. Life was never boring.

People made life interesting! For example, we served the man with two thumbs on one hand and the woman with eleven children and a drunken husband. We even had a bully for a customer.

My father tamed the bully. The bully would grab bags of chips from the younger children and hit them when they tried to hang on to their chips. His swearing was intentionally loud to terrify the children. They were brave when they refused to hand over their meal. His game was intimidation as he attempted to rob them! 'Give me or else' was his usual theme!

One night my father asked the bully if he would like a free fish supper. Of course a huge smile formed on his face at the thought!

The bait was on the hook!

Now you have to understand my father's hands were as tough as leather after years of hard, physical work. Initially he was a miner after leaving school. He worked as a car mechanic at night after a hard day down the mine. Later when he developed health issues he decided he would use his pioneering skills and designed and made a Bedford van into a mobile fish and chip van. He also made the stainless steel fryers from scratch too. Once he knew how to do one, he made others. People from all over Scotland would come and he would help them set up in the mobile fish and chip business in their area.

The bully was delighted at the offer of a free fish supper. The only thing was, the bully had to take the fish out my father's hand and he had just taken the fish straight out of the hot fat! My father pressed the newly cooked, piping hot fish tightly in the bully's hand. The children laughed as my dad told the bully he would let go if he promised to leave the 'weans' alone! The dancing bully duly screamed that he would leave them alone. Nano seconds later he got his free fish supper. He kept his promise! After his encounter with a hot fish, the bully left the weans alone!

Life was good.

We got our pocket money every week, a paper bag full of salty halfpennies. We were thrilled to bits.

As good as life was, I had a terrible dark secret which affected me deeply. I told no one. I could not physically open my mouth to tell anyone and if I did, I had no words to describe this darkness. Not for thirty years anyway! More of that later!

I used to wonder, "Who am I? Why am I like this? Why me?"

I was very quiet and exceptionally shy. I did not like being the centre of attention. It was painful. I did not like men and found it hard to look them in the eye.

I remember on my 21st birthday going to Glasgow for a haircut and a new dress and coming back to a full house. A surprise party had been organised with aunts, uncles, and cousins. My mother had to coax me and eventually pull me into the living room where everyone was waiting. I wanted to run a mile. I hated everyone looking at me.

As a child I always played my favourite game. I was the teacher and my two sisters were the pupils. We had doll bunk beds which we turned on their ends and used as desks in my dad's empty garage which was our classroom. Brilliant fun! We played for hours.

I remember one day a neighbour's daughter wanted to play school with us. I could not believe how naughty, disruptive and disobedient she was. As the teacher I had to use the 'belt'. So I went outside and fetched it. When I came back her behaviour was worse, so I told her to hold out her hand. I used my 'belt' on her. I ran the bunch of nettles I had pulled, up and down her bare forearm! Both she and I suffered. I more than she when my mother found out what I had done!

After the chip vans, my father bought a shop, a general greengrocers, in the neighbouring village of Holytown. Early rises, sorting the newspapers ready to be collected by the regular customers and serving in the shop at weekends till 8pm, were new experiences. Again we met so many people. My sister met her future husband while serving in the shop. There were so many laughs!

I used to sew skirts and dresses. One day while I was going up the ladder in the shop to fetch something from the top shelf, I had the weirdest experience of climbing up but falling down at the same time! It wasn't till my home made skirt landed around my ankles that I knew what had happened! The queue of customers had a good laugh while I was duly embarrassed.

Another time I happened to catch a couple of teenage boys stealing from a display stand in the middle of the shop. I was so annoyed at their brazenness that I shouted, "Put that back or I'll... " I stuttered nervously not really knowing what to say next. They answered defiantly, "Or you'll what?". "Or...or I'll... I'll tickle your neck!" I blurted out. I did not live that down for years.

I remember the Pakistani lady, who could not speak English, buying tins of dog food for her dog. We discovered later she had no dog. She thought the dog food was stew and had been feeding her family with it! Later when she began to speak more English, and feeling rather pleased with herself at the improvement in her vocabulary, she came in one day and confidently asked for a can opener. I duly gave her the can opener to be told "NO" rather emphatically! It took more than five minutes of me showing her a whole variety of kitchen utensils before I discovered she wanted an egg whisk! She learned a new word!

I went to Hamilton College and graduated as a teacher in 1977. There were 400 in my graduation year and no jobs for many of us after we graduated. I got a drama job from August till October going round local primary schools in North Lanarkshire using drama to teach history. I was 'Black Buffalo' and we taught about Red Indians and their way of life. That was a fun time.

After the October holiday I got a job in Clarkston Primary in Airdrie. I loved teaching there. The headmaster was a unique person. He was one in a million; Mr William Brown. It was while teaching there that two significant things happened.

My sister and her friend were going to church one Sunday morning and they invited me to join them. That first Sunday morning I sat at the back of the local Church of Scotland and stared at the stained glass window at the front of the church. It depicted a New Testament Jesus in a tunic with a modern day boy and girl on each side of Him. Jesus had a hand on each of their heads.

A sudden question resonated deep within me. "Was Jesus real?"

It was followed by another question. "Did Jesus really live?"

Slowly, I realised that for all the times I taught the Christmas and Easter story, Jesus was more of a fairy tale character to me than a real person who had actually lived on this earth.

After this I started going to church regularly. I volunteered to help at the Sunday school, then the Guides, then the Bible Class, later on at the Youth Fellowship. I even volunteered to clean the church on a Thursday night, much to the minister's surprise! No one else had ever asked him before to clean the toilets. I loved helping to clean the building.

During Holy Week at Easter I would take a slot in the weekly programme of looking after the church while it was open to visitors. I would take a whole pile of school work in to do in the room at the back of the church. The minister would look at me disappointed somehow. It was not till years later that I understood. He wanted me to spend time meditating on the Easter story. That was the whole reason for the church being open during Holy Week. I am afraid to say it was all totally lost on me then.

The second significant thing to happen was that my mother became ill. She had gone to the doctors on numerous occasions saying there was something wrong with her stomach. To most people they could clearly see there was something far wrong because of the way her stomach swelled up, but the doctor could find nothing.

She was finally diagnosed with cancer. She was operated on for eight hours, lost six gallons of fluid and six stone of cancerous warts were removed. Chemotherapy followed.

My mother had worked as hard as my father for years. She had worked as a nurse before having us. As well as looking after all of us and the house, she washed all the white aprons and overalls after the chip vans returned anytime between midnight and 2 a.m., followed by washing the vans' greasy floors. I did not know it at the time but she was a Proverbs 31 woman, wife and mother in every respect. When we were young she would rise early when my dad went to the pit and sew all our clothes; dresses, jackets, coats and blouses, making us three girls all have matching outfits.

I was afraid of losing my mother. I decided to find out what happens after you die. I asked the minister to help me. He gave me a huge, heavy book called a concordance and showed me how to use it. He gave me other books as well. I decided to study what the Bible says about heaven and hell, life and death. It was simple for me, for I reckoned if my car needed fixing I would take it to a garage. If my body was sick I would visit a doctor. So the church and the Bible needed to be used in my investigation into the truth of eternal issues.

A huge list of every Scripture verse I could find relating to my topics was made. I came to a simple conclusion. If heaven and hell existed I would prefer heaven thank you very much! So from that point on, I did good works by the ton. I figured if I wanted to get to heaven, I would work hard, do good deeds and God would see and reward me with entry to heaven. I felt good but I still did not really know if there was a heaven and hell, but just in case there was I was keeping my options open!

I became a Ranger Guide Leader and a district commissioner of North Lanarkshire Guides. I joined the church and went through adult baptism. I knelt on the cushion at the front of the church quietly saying to myself, "There must be more than this."

Later I became Hamilton Presbytery's Bible Class Advisor and also one of the first of four woman elders in the church. I was enjoying myself in church and with church things yet somehow God seemed far away.

During these years I was watching my mother's illness worsen.

She told me not to worry about her because she knew she was heaven bound and did not fear death.

She said, "I know where I am going. What about you?"

Exactly! What about me?

About five years after her first cancer operation, she became ill again. This time the doctor diagnosed gall bladder trouble. When they operated they discovered cancer everywhere and simply stitched her back up. She died in the recovery room of Hairmyres Hospital. She was only forty nine years old. The day she died was also the day of my brother's wedding. My mother must have known for she made my brother promise that no matter what happened to her, his wedding must go ahead.

Go ahead it did! Valium helped my dad through the day and the rest of us just did it anyway putting the 'Dow steel' into action. After the wedding, my dad and I took my mum's cousin, Rita, home to Uddingston about five miles away. I cried quietly as they chatted in the back seat. I kept saying my car had a problem as it wasn't going fast. It was only when I got home I discovered the reason. I was in first gear the whole journey there and back!

The day of the funeral came. We were sitting in the crematorium and the minister was speaking. I was so numb, however, I didn't really hear what he was saying.

"And God is a God of love."

I heard that!

Internally I screamed, yelling at God in a bottled rage, "You – a God of Love? You took my mum. She died a horrifically painful death. She was only forty nine! Look at murderers and others that exist, yet You took my mum. She was good!"

Suddenly a memory lunged to the fore of my screaming mind. My mother had said "Don't worry about me I know where I am going. What about you?"

What about me! If I died today where would I spend eternity? My mother knew for certain she was going to heaven. At least she was at peace. I believed she was in heaven but that knowledge did not help my heartache one bit!

I remembered a few months earlier when I was on my way to London and was standing at Buchanan Street bus station in Glasgow, a voice in my head simply said, "You hope to go to London but if you get on the Inverness bus you won't get to London. It's the wrong destination."

What would happen if I spent my whole life hoping to go to heaven and ended up in hell after death? I sat there hoping to go to heaven; I sat there wishing to know, like my mum, where I was going after death. I realised hoping was not enough. I needed to really know for certain!

Again I screamed silently to God, "Show me You're a God of love."

Suddenly, what felt like a light blanket of comforting love fell all over me and I felt such a tangible peace.

At the same time I felt arms go round me and I was comforted to the depth of my being. I had been crying uncontrollably, my heart breaking at the thought I would not see my mother again. Then when this strange but beautiful love touched me, the crying stopped as peace completely flooded me. I looked at my father. He had not moved. Yet the arms holding me were real, loving, comforting! I was not delusional.

It was at that point that I heard a voice, strong, loving and kind, say:

"Now do you believe I AM?"

Wow! I knew God had touched me. I knew God had spoken. I had felt Him and heard Him. I knew that I knew that I knew God was real.

The only problem was He was still a million miles away, until I met Him in Troon a year later.

I was led by an incredible set of circumstances to be part of a Church of Scotland Summer mission team to Troon.

There were fifty four adults and some children. I had never gone on a mission before and was told that the format was the same for every mission: prayers, breakfast, and kids' games down on the beach or in a park, followed by lunch and afternoon games. Evening meal was followed by fishing, whatever that was, then the evening programme.

I arrived on the Sunday of a two-week mission to be met by the cheery minister in charge. He welcomed me warmly and then asked, "Are you a Christian?"

"Of course," I replied confidently.

"How do you know you are a Christian?" he continued.

"Well," thinking quickly," I go to church, help with the children's Sunday school and sometimes read my Bible."

I thought this was a good answer. He burst my bubble immediately by saying, "So, going to church and sometimes reading your Bible makes you a Christian does it? You and I will have a chat later."

Now I was an easy going type of person, kind and caring but also quiet and shy. But when he said this, I knew he knew something I didn't know and an intense desire rose up within me to reorganise his face on the wall behind him!

Whatever was happening to me? The minister asked me to do morning prayers next day at 8.00 a.m. What were morning prayers and how do you 'do' them? I bought a notebook and page after page, line after line I tried to write morning prayers, only to rip each page off the spiral and discard each one in the bin. I realised I didn't know what to say or do.

Monday morning came and my turn to do morning prayers. There hadn't been time to copy anyone else's morning prayers, so I spoke hesitantly reading my insecure scribble on half a page of the much thinner notebook.

Never before had I known the certainty of my words reaching the ceiling and landing back down on my head! Something was flat and empty. It was me! I also knew everyone else knew that too!

The week consisted of morning prayers, Bible study, lunch, beach games and children's talks in the afternoon. Then it was tea, followed by fishing and the outreach meeting, just as I had been told.

Food was interesting. We only ate what the church holding the mission provided. One meal was simply a banana! It made me realise that certain people had no idea what going on a mission was like. I supposed that if they were given just a banana for their tea they would have something to say!

The week progressed quickly till it came to Thursday night. I was teamed up with a young teenage girl who had been on many missions. We went out in pairs covering specific areas of Troon to fish.

I hated fishing. Each night we were to walk up to total strangers on the streets and invite them back to the church evening outreach meeting. No one I had asked so far had come, so I wasn't expecting that night to be any different. It was Thursday and we were allocated Troon Cross to fish.

We walked slowly down the street. I was busy telling my partner, Linda, that, as she was the more experienced, she should do the asking. I was told politely 'No' the only way to learn was to do it! Such wisdom from a teenager! How annoying!

Not what I wanted to hear.

We came upon a group of bikers standing in a crowd wearing their very 'in' Doctor Who scarves, long multi-coloured striped woollen scarves wrapped several times round their necks, trailing down their backs. No health and safety rules in those days. There were about twenty of them. They stood beside their motorbikes chatting and larking around.

As we were now standing in front of them, one of the bikers barked, "What do you want?"

As my partner refused to answer, I realised I would have to reply. I hesitantly whispered, "Would you like to come to the church tonight?"

The leader replied, "What! You are asking if we would like to go to church!" Mocking looks stared back at us.

"What about it guys? Shall we go?"

Before we knew it, we felt like the Pied Piper of Hamelin, walking to the church with a large group of bikers following behind. All I could think was, "Brilliant! We've caught some fish and it's only 6.50pm!

We can sit in the Café and chat before the evening meeting begins at 7.30pm." Our fishing was over for the night. Then I heard one the leaders say, "Well done girls we'll take over from here. You can go back out and fish as there's still time."

We did go back out but caught no fish.

The evening meeting started. I was sitting next to a biker. A young 16-year-old girl stood up at the testimony time and said, "The day I met Jesus, my life changed."

Don't be silly I thought. How can anyone meet Jesus? He's dead!

An old man stood up in the audience and started shouting out questions, interrupting her as she spoke. I was gobsmacked and felt terrible for the 16 year old. I need not have worried for she gave brilliant answers to his every question. It came across quite clearly that she knew Jesus!

After the girl spoke, a drama group from St. Andrew's University performed a simple sketch.

A man came in and sat down to read his newspaper. A knock was heard and before he answered the door, he shouted and asked, "Who is there?"

The voice off stage said, "Jesus!"

The man lowered his paper and said, "Jesus, I have my whole life ahead of me I certainly don't want to have anything to do with You. I am young and I want to enjoy my life, not go to church!".

Time passes.

The man sat and told us his life was good. He had married, had two children and a great job. He was happy. That was evident.

Again a knock was heard.

He shouted, "Who is it?"

"Jesus."

The man said that he now knew all about Jesus. He had heard how Jesus died for his sins to be forgiven. He had even heard how Jesus is the way to heaven. But he was enjoying his life and asked if Jesus could come back when he was much older.

The man sat and read his newspaper, suddenly he froze with his face showing agonising pain, made a sound as he clutched his heart, slipped to the floor and remained very still. We knew he had died.

Everyone thought the sketch was over so they started clapping. The man however was still on the floor, not moving! There was a long awkward silence as the audience was unsure what to do.

Slowly the man got off the floor, looked around him fearfully and stuttered rather hysterically, "It is pitch darkness in here. I am frightened. Where am I? Is that a door?"

He started banging on the door, shouting, "Jesus, are You there? Please let me out of this terrible place."

A loud, strong voice is heard. "I never knew you!"

My heart missed a beat at the finality of the sketch. It was obvious for that man it was too late. The consequences were too terrible to contemplate!

The minister then stood up after this and spoke of knowing about Jesus or actually knowing Jesus and the difference between these two statements. I sat and acknowledged I knew about Jesus but I didn't know Him. How could I? He was dead!

The minister then spoke about a thing called sin that is in every one of us when we are born and how this separates us from God. He told us sin puts ourselves first so that we do whatever we want. He spoke about how God loves us so much and how as He is holy, He has to punish sin.

He quoted Scripture verses from Romans 3:23, "All have sinned and fall short of the glory of God" and Romans 6:23 "For the wages of sin is death". Not exactly something I wanted to hear! The Good News followed with "but the gift of God is eternal life in Christ Jesus our Lord."

Now that was indeed good news! He sent Jesus His Son to die for our sins. Jesus, God's Son, paid the price for our sins by taking the punishment meant for us upon His own body. We needed to respond to His gift of salvation by thanking Jesus for dying for us and asking Him to forgive us our sins and invite Him to live in us as our Lord and Saviour.

As the minister spoke I saw an unusual picture on the wall behind him. It was of a huge tree trunk, ripped down the middle and made into a cross.

I turned to the biker beside me, commenting on the picture on the wall behind the minister. He simply said there was no picture. I was seeing things. But I knew there was a cross before me even if no one else could see it! When I looked at it again, I nearly fainted! The minister was saying, "If you were the only person living Jesus would still have to die for you because only the blood of Jesus can wash all our sins away and enable us to gain entrance into heaven!

He pointed at me as he said this and I looked up again at the cross on the wall. It was still there, only this time I saw my name written horizontally across the tree in huge bold black letters "MAY DOW."

I knew in that instant that Jesus Christ had died for MY sin.

The minister was now asking us to respond to what Jesus had done for us all. He invited all who wanted to know Jesus to come and say a prayer of salvation. He showed how easy this was by offering a huge box of Milk Tray chocolates to anyone who would come and take them.

Now I loved Milk Tray but to walk out in front of everyone and simply take them was just too difficult. My fear of people looking at me ruled again. How long would I suffer from this debilitating condition?

Only a small boy in the front row took the chocolates and promptly told his mother that they were his as he had taken them. No other person had responded to the invitation to take the gift on offer.

The minister then prayed. I wanted to but I was assailed by flashing thoughts through my mind, "Your minister back home doesn't talk like this. This is not right. Don't say that prayer."

So I didn't, even though my heart was beating so fast and loud I thought it would burst.

I went to bed that night without speaking to anyone about the events which had occurred at the evening meeting. I put my head on my pillow, as I lay down on the church hall floor, I absolutely knew because I had not said YES to Jesus, I had said NO and because I had not asked Him to forgive me my sins and had not received His gift of salvation, if I died that night I knew that I knew for certain, that I was bound for hell!

I was distraught!

Hysterical actually!

It was too late to respond to Jesus. I realised that He had come to me earlier in the evening at the end of the meeting, and I had said 'No' because I had refused to say 'Yes!'

I felt terrible. I was crying loudly disturbing those around me. A friend I had met at the mission asked me to come with her to the church kitchen. I was in such agony of soul. We talked. I was ready to get right with God.

I prayed a simple prayer. "Lord I know I am a sinner and that Jesus died in my place for my sin. Please forgive me my sin and come into my life as Lord and Saviour. Thank You Jesus. Amen." Those words said sincerely changed my eternal destination. They changed my entire life!

I knew for certain I was no longer bound for hell. I was bound for heaven. I knew it as a true fact. I no longer wondered if there was a heaven or if there was a hell. I knew, but I knew, but I knew I was heaven bound and that hell had been avoided!

It was July 9th 1982 at 2.10 a.m. It was my second birthday, the one that ensures my entrance to heaven.

Next morning at morning prayers, the minister asked me to share what had happened to me. Naturally there was no way I was going to stand in front all of these people and speak. So I simply shook my head and declined his offer. However everyone strongly encouraged me and eventually I stood up and walked to the front of the room. My face was as red as a beetroot, as I shared that I had come to the mission with a bit missing in my life. I found Jesus. He was what had been missing all along! They clapped.

Next day, as I walked along this particular street not far from Troon Cross, I heard a voice behind me say, "I will make you a fisher of men." I looked behind me but there was no one there. "Strange", I thought. I walked on and heard the same voice again say, "I will make you a fisher of men."

Whatever did that mean? I had not a clue as, to be honest, it sounded a bit double Dutch to me at the time!

To this day I can stand on the exact spot on the pavement where I heard those words all those years ago. It seems to have an invisible cross marked on it.

I was soon to find out just what a fisher of men was!

Happy Birthday indeed!

Early Years as a Christian

When I returned home from mission, the minister phoned and asked me to come and tell him all about being on mission.

I told the minister everything. I told him about the daily mission routine. I especially told him, rather excitedly, the part where I became a Christian. He looked at me oddly. So I told him how I got saved, and was born again and got converted. I thought perhaps he didn't know what I was talking about so I used all the new terms I had learned for becoming a Christian.

His reply rather took me by surprise, "You didn't need to do that. You were OK as you were."

I felt I had done something seriously wrong. He was the minister after all and was a very well educated man.

I went to bed that night praying and asking God to forgive me for saying the prayer asking Jesus to be Lord of my life.

How I wished I hadn't prayed that prayer. I felt confused and sad. My joy had gone.

During the night, I saw a very bright light coming up the steep stairs towards my open attic bedroom door. I was scared and hid under my covers. Peeking out, I saw there was a form standing at the doorway in the midst of the white light.

A voice stated rather authoritatively, "Nevertheless I am not ashamed: for I know whom I have believed, and am persuaded that He is able to keep that which I have committed unto Him against that day." Then the light and the form simply vanished.

Next morning I nearly fainted when I read the next part of my daily Bible reading.

2 Timothy 1:12 said, *"For I know whom I have believed, and am persuaded that He is able to keep what I have committed to Him until that day."*

Was it an angel who had visited me and given me a word from God? Or was it the Lord Himself? I did not know, but from that moment on I was determined to go with what God said.

I prayed for the Lord to forgive me for doubting Him. I knew I had been hell bound and I now knew for certain I was heaven bound. No more would I doubt that truth or allow anyone to rob me of the assurance I had.

Within hours of giving my life to God I was hearing Him speak to me. Everyone said I was different.

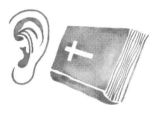

It was arranged for me to spend some time with my cousin and her husband in Strichen near Fraserburgh.

I sang 'Hallelujah' all the way there, a journey of just over three hours in my little brown mini. Hallelujah rang loudly out of the depth of my being. I was filled with an incredible joy and sang one word a hundred different ways. Some tunes were from the Church of Scotland hymnbook, others were tunes I made up. I could have flown to Strichen as Hallelujahs made me high!

One day during my time there, my cousin had to go to her lawyer's on business so she and her husband dropped me off at the beach. I sat reading a book I had grabbed from my book shelf before I left. I had had it for a couple of years and never read it. I sat happily in the sun just reading.

I remember reading Chapter 3 about occult practices keeping us from drawing close to God and really knowing Him. I read a long list of occult practices like Ouija board, fortune-telling, mediums, spiritualism, palm reading, horoscopes, psychic readings, séance, crystal ball reading and found myself saying out loud, "I've done that and that and that!"

My father's old aunt stayed with us before my mother died. She was a numerologist, enjoying her crystal ball, tea cup reading and horoscopes. It was she who got me very interested in the occult; something I didn't fully understand at the time.

In this third chapter of the book, it mentioned all the things I had tried. I had even paid a fortune to try and discover my future using them. At college I had done an assignment on spiritualism. I got an A!

As I sat on the beach, this book explained about Satan and occult practices. It described the power of any involvement in these as negative, harmful and even destructive to those participating; including being under a curse. I read Deuteronomy 18:10-11 which said "one who practices witchcraft, or a soothsayer, or one who interprets omens, or a sorcerer, or one who conjures spells, or a medium, or a spiritist, or one who calls up the dead. For all who do these things are an abomination to the LORD".

I swallowed hard as I did not like the thought of being an abomination to God because I had done these things. Leviticus 19:31, "Give no regard to mediums and familiar spirits; do not seek after them, to be defiled by them: I am the LORD your God." Leviticus 20:6 "And the person who turns to mediums and familiar spirits, to prostitute himself with them, I will set My face against that person."

I read this chapter as a piece of information. I knew now these practices were an abomination to God. I knew they defiled us. I was glad that that was my old life, which was gone.

2 Corinthians 5:17 says, *"Therefore, if anyone is in Christ, he is a new creation; old things have passed away; behold, all things have become new."* This was me. I had been born again into the family of God and I knew it as absolute truth!

The chapter finished with a prayer of repentance for having been involved in one or any of the practices on the occult list. I read the prayer and started to read chapter 4.

I tried to get past the first paragraph, I physically could not! No matter how often I attempted to get onto paragraph 2, I physically could not read one word.

"What's wrong? This is weird!" I thought sitting on the beach.

A voice came into my head, "Don't just read that prayer. Pray it sincerely."

So I went back to the end of chapter 3 and prayed that prayer as sincerely as I could.

I meant every word. I repented of my interest in and my participation in all those occult practices mentioned. I felt free somehow!

I continued and read the rest of the book with no further interruptions.

When I returned from my holiday I heard God's voice again. When praying, it was impressed upon me to write letters to people asking them to forgive me for various things I had done to them over the years. Over the next weeks I ended up writing forty two letters attempting to put things right. I also took back library books I had kept and I paid the late returned fee too. Many people forgave me and told me not to worry but the majority did not reply or say anything. All I knew was I was being obedient. I was being taught restitution. Genuine repentance leads to a desire to redress wrongs.

For years, on Tuesdays, my mother had two magazines delivered, Woman and Woman's Own. They continued to be delivered after she had died. I thought they were brilliant and I loved a Tuesday to see them lying there when I came home from work. God very simply said "Cancel those and don't read them." So I did.

I would hear Him say, "Don't listen to pop songs...Go visit... or read this Bible story or have a summer mission for the children in the village. Go on mission. I would hear, clean the church, and take Mary for a run in the car."

Mary was an old lady with special needs I had met while doing a summer holiday job in a geriatric hospital in Shotts. She had been in the hospital for thirty six years and as far as we knew had no relatives. No one ever visited her. I would clean the wards and chat as I did so. She was in an individual room and it looked so institutionalised that I asked if pictures could be put up on the walls to try and brighten it up a bit. She liked her new room!

It was summer and as it was warm, she sat in her wheelchair outside in the shaded area at the end of her long corridor. She loved it. She would speak to me, not clearly, but enough to be understood. No one knew she could speak! No one believed she could speak till they heard her. I gave her a colouring book to occupy her time and she enjoyed this for a while. However, she decided she would draw her own pictures! These were then put up on her walls. She was really pleased with her accomplishments. The other ladies in the other wards asked if they too could have pictures on their ward walls, so that was arranged also. Kind deeds are contagious.

When I left the job I continued to visit Mary for seven years every Sunday after church, except when away on holiday.

There was an old man in the church I used to sit beside, who was lonely and so I took him as well as some of the Bible class to visit Mary every Sunday. They immediately hit it off.

One day I decided to ask permission to take her for a run in the car to a local loch. Permission was duly granted and off we set. I thought a new experience she would enjoy, would be to take the car through a car wash. So we visited one near the hospital. An explanation of what would happen was given before we went into the car wash. She sat excitedly laughing and giggling then all of a sudden it changed to screaming! What was wrong? Without my knowledge she had opened her window, enabling her and the seat to be soaked! Our first day out had lasted all of fifteen minutes. She had to go back and have her clothes changed and her trip for the day was over!

At her funeral, apart from the local minister, there was her nephew, a doctor from Paisley and the staff nurse and me. It was so sad but I knew she was in a far better place.

The journey following Jesus is an amazing learning curve.

Every month my parents' insurance woman would come on an evening to collect the money. She had lost her husband, and had to find work she could do in the evenings.

She loved to chat as she found days were taken up with her two young children. Often she stayed for a couple of hours, business over within the first five minutes.

On this particular visit, my parents were out. I was not long born again. The film 'Stars Wars' was being shown on TV for the first time. I had not seen it at the cinema and I was really looking forward to it. Knock. Knock. Who's there? The insurance woman of course, just as the film started.

I am ashamed to say, I was not amused! In she came, blethering away as usual. I, however, half listened because I was trying my hardest to watch Star Wars. Normally the T.V. would have been instantly switched off whenever people were visiting.

All of a sudden she said, "I have just been diagnosed with cancer and am really frightened!" God rebuked me instantly. She had my full attention much later than she should have! I turned off the film and listened. I did my best to share the Good News of Jesus with her. Death is not the end. It's a doorway into eternity and heaven. That word cancer is really frightening as it holds its captives in fear and torment. I don't know if she responded to Jesus' gift of eternal life or not. She passed away not long afterwards. I have never been able to watch Star Wars as it brings back bad memories of my wilful selfishness and disobedience.

I was ignorant of so much but step by step He led me and taught me and helped me.

One Sunday morning as I dropped twenty pence into the offering plate I heard, "You have just offered me the price of a packet of crisps!" That seemed so inappropriate!

Just after this, the Bible class were invited to an event in Coatbridge. Guess what the lady minister spoke on? Tithing! Malachi 3:10"Bring all the tithes into the storehouse, that there may be food in My house, and try Me now in this," says the LORD of hosts, "If I will not open for you the windows of heaven and pour out for you such blessing that there will not be room enough to receive it."

She lined up ten children and gave them each an apple. She asked for one apple to be given to God. We saw the nine that were left. It looked such a lot that we had all to ourselves. Surely God was worth one!

Needless to say I finally got the message.

He showed me how to give a tithe or a tenth of my wages to Him. After all He died in my place and set me free from the fear of death and hell! I was left with nine tenths for my own needs and wants. A tenth does not seem much when you have it all clearly revealed to you.

Hearing what God was saying did not always go down well with me. My friends were planning to go to a disco in Edinburgh. It was a young farmers' disco being held on January 26th. For months I had firmly stated that I did not want to go. However, on the day in question at the last minute I gave in and said that I would go. I heard very clearly from heaven. "Do not go."

What did I do? I went ahead and got dressed up for a night at a disco.

Normally I would wear a nice dress but I remember putting on thick woollen tights and my boots and a thick cardigan and my heavy jacket. I did not look as if I was going to a disco but rather a walk in the countryside!

My three friends and I got into my friend Jean's estate car and headed for Edinburgh. It was a cold frosty evening. When we arrived at the venue we were surprised to find it practically empty as there was a new venue which had recently opened up nearby. This was a very different night indeed. Due to numbers being considerably depleted the place was freezing and we sat and shivered till we came to our senses and decided to move on.

We walked carefully to the car park watching how we walked as the ground was slippery. I looked up and noticed the clear sky and beautiful stars. It was a very cold crisp night. I noted mentally that the roads would be slippery too. We had not gone very far when we skidded on ice and after swerving all over the road, we ended up going off the road and down an embankment!

The car was nose first down the embankment and we struggled to get out of the car because it was lying at such a strange angle. It was freezing; however as I was not dressed for a disco, compared to my friends, I was relatively warm and comfortable and not shivering.

We waited for the police. When they came we packed into the back seat of their car trying to keep warm. Our car was towed out. It was fine for driving home.

After travelling for a few miles, we suddenly heard and felt a loud bang and crash. Sitting in the front seat, all I saw was the windscreen fill with a view of the sky! Where was the road?

It felt as if my very breath was being forced out of my lungs. It was a very dark, frightening moment. All I could do was force out the name of Jesus with great difficulty.

"Jesus! Jesus! Jesus!" I automatically whispered because I was in such pain. In my ignorance, I didn't know what the Bible said in Psalm 50:15 "Call upon Me in the day of trouble; I will rescue you..."

Another loud bump and this time we saw the car was skidding all over the road, finally coming to a stop at the side of the road. Shaken we got out of the car. When we looked behind us we saw a bread van. The van had hit us. The windows of my friend Jean's car were smashed and glass was everywhere.

Walking towards the van behind us, I noticed that the driver was swapping seats with his passenger. I asked the men what had happened. The man who had been the passenger said he was the driver and that he had hit black ice. I could smell drink from the original driver; now the passenger! They were told in no uncertain terms that we knew they had swapped places.

He said, "Please don't tell anyone. I was told if I had another crash I would lose my job."

At that moment the police came and heard our version of the story and theirs!

After taking a statement, the police officers took us to Monklands Hospital where we were later released with cuts and bruises. The police even took us home, something they do not normally do. I got in that morning about 8 a.m. to be asked by my father, "Did you have a good time, hen?"

I went upstairs to my bedroom thanking God for my escapes.

I read my daily reading notes for the new day.

I was amazed to read Psalm 91. The little story in Our Daily Bread notes said, "wasn't it good to know that during this winter season of slippery roads and pavements, God is able to help us stay safe? The verse quoted was Psalm 91:11-12 "For He shall give His angels charge over you, to keep you in all your ways. In their hands they shall bear you up, lest you dash your foot against a stone."

I knew, but I knew that God had saved us. The only thing I experienced was whiplash. I could have avoided these two incidents if I had only been obedient to stay at home!

I was blown away with how God was letting me know again and again, He really does know me and He really looks after me and cares for me. Once again He showed me the absolute relevance of the Bible truth, speaking into my situation so exactly. Amazing!

As I was learning all these new truths, I just had to tell everyone about my "born again experience."

I had the Bible Class to teach; I shared the Good News with them. One by one, they too accepted Jesus as Saviour. A church prayer meeting, which was open to everyone, was started before the morning service.

My friend Jean and I started a drama group. We wrote sketches and performed them in local churches,

Women's Guilds and youth groups. It was great fun and the fellowship we enjoyed was special. We used to rehearse on Wednesday evenings. If we needed an extra car to take us to a venue, my mum's cousin, Edith, and a friend were duly conscripted!

Once we visited a particular church in Blantyre with new sketches.

One was called 'The Moaner': A church member goes into church, sits down and moans about everything. She comments on things like the flower arrangements.

"A blind man could do better!"

The Minister's hair got it next.

"You could fry an egg on that greasy head of hair!

At the end when we joined the queue for tea and coffee, this strong tap on my shoulder made me turn round to see one very unhappy woman.

"And just what is wrong with my flower arranging?"

The minister then joined me and said that he knew everyone commented on his greasy hair and that he did not wash his hair deliberately to annoy the congregation and give them something to talk about!

God does know how to hit the nail on the head!

It was decided the Bible Class would go away for the weekend. The Church of Scotland had a Conference centre in Skelmorlie called Stroove House. We went there regularly for weekends and then we decided to go for a week during the summer. I also took the school Scripture Union group there for weekends.

The first time the Bible Class wanted to go for a week, a single coach was organised to take thirty six teenagers from my church and a friend's church in Coatbridge. Just before we were due to go, I was told there would be no forty-seater bus!

To the natural mind another bus could easily be acquired. But no, none was available. I simply knew that no matter what, we would have this holiday with these two Bible classes. I prayed like mad asking for God to make a way.

The local community 12-seater minibus was available, so after phoning Alan, the oldest boy, and phoning round everyone making new arrangements, it was decided he go first with the first group and get set up for lunch.

So I picked up the first group at 7.00 a.m. and an hour later we were in Skelmorlie.

Next I drove the hour long journey back to collect the next group of children. It took three hour-long journeys there and back to get the kids to Stroove House before lunch was served that day.

Our holiday consisted of praise and worship, Bible teaching, prayer, fun, plenty of food and chores and next to no sleep! It was an eye opener seeing how the kids approached things. The first time one new teen was asked to dry the dishes, the dish towel was picked up dangling between two fingers and a, "What does one do with this?" was uttered. One duly got shown what one does with this! An expert dish drier went home from her time at Skelmorlie.

We would go to Stroove many times over the next number of years at Easter, summer, September weekends or the October breaks. It was a great time working with those teenagers.

There were plenty of opportunities to share fun times serving Jesus at home too.

On a Saturday morning, for example, wearing old clothes and gloves we would turn up at church. We'd split into teams and slide under pews cleaning the floor, dusting the pew ledges and polishing the parquet flooring as we raced to the front of the church and back!

The afternoon was then spent going somewhere nice.

I heard God simply say, "Invite lonely old folk to Christmas dinner."

With the help of local people we were given a list of names. We had great discussions about what the menu would be and what to give them as gifts. Parents and family friends helped in those days and everyone worked really hard to make things happen. No 'health and safety' rules in those days and we managed very well.

Again God spoke and said, "Have a mission for kids."

The Bible class were the leaders. We put the word out. The mission consisted of games, arts n'crafts and Bible choruses and stories.

Local children actually came. Everyone worked really hard and before we knew it, the mission was over.

I knew a group of intellectually disadvantaged adults from Airdrie. Their ages ranged from 18 to 64, male and female. I used to visit them after school as their hostel was five minutes away from where I worked. In those days, apart from going to the day centre, they mainly existed as a large self-contained family with the matron as a mother figure. Life was slow and quiet!

Again I heard God say to bring them to the church and have a special day of activities.

Permission was given from the matron, the mini bus was hired and we were ready to bring them into the church hall. We packed the programme with all kinds of new experiences for them to try.

They loved arts and crafts, choruses and Bible stories as well as the food, of course.

The Special Saturdays grew into weekends away and soon we tried a week away with them and the Bible Class.

We hired the Arbroath Baptist Centre for these holidays.

Again holiday was spelled HARD WORK but there was no denying the laughter and fellowship we all enjoyed.

The circus was on one night in Arbroath and we took everyone along. David, a sixty- something hostel friend, had always wanted to see a camel. He was beside himself when a camel walked silently over the sawdust and literally put its face right up to his nose. What a delight to see his face! He talked about it for ages afterwards.

One holiday we focused on the name of Jesus as a teaching topic. Caroline, one of the girls, went into the chip shop and asked for a bag of chips in Jesus' name please!

Another time, one of the Bible class teenagers, burst into my room about 2 a.m. She woke me up as she knelt beside my bed and said to one very shattered leader, "Smell my breath!"

Truly you have to be ready for anything when you follow Jesus. I duly smelled her breath. Actually I had no option as she was in my face!

"Carbolic soap!" I uttered mystified.

"Have you been eating carbolic soap?"

Now I have to add that earlier that day she had come and asked for prayer as she was a secret smoker and was terrified her mother would find out and duly kill her!

I prayed that God would do something to stop her from taking her next cigarette!

This was His answer!

When she lit up all she could taste was carbolic soap.

Truly God's ways are not our ways as the Bible says in Isaiah 55:8 "For My thoughts are not your thoughts, nor are your ways My ways," says the LORD. "For as the heavens are higher than the earth, so are My ways higher than your ways, and My thoughts than your thoughts."

It was another learning experience that God can do anything. I was to experience time and time again just what God can do!

I felt God asked me to give Him my school summer holidays. So I volunteered to do a Scripture Union camp for a week. Again it was a huge learning curve but highly enjoyable doing archery, swimming, arts and crafts and many other things with the girls and leaders. At the end of this it was my Bible Class week in Arbroath.

When this was finished, it was mission fortnight with the Church of Scotland in Ayrshire near Turnberry. This was the first time I did 'door to door visiting.' Another 'thrown in at the deep end' activity! Not really a joy to be experienced, more a case of an experience being endured.

"It's simple," said the leader. "You go round the street, praying and knocking on every door asking to share the Good News with the occupant."

"Simple?" I whispered scathingly. The reality was that most of the time the people were not interested in hearing about Jesus. They politely or otherwise told us what they thought or where we should go!

"Remember it is not you they are rejecting. It's Jesus in you." True perhaps I know, but to be honest, it still hurt.

But the absolute joy when a divine appointment answers the door!

It's as if they have a neon light above their head, "This is the one!"

Talk about open, hungry, seeking! The lady prayed her way into heaven that summer night in Maybole. She had been reading her son's Bible and asking how to know

God. The change in her face was obvious and instantaneous.

I was literally hooked!

It was amazing the way a simple but life-transforming prayer had the power to change eternal destinies as well as physical appearances! It worked for me. It works for everyone.

I felt as if that summer had lasted for months. I felt enriched, abundantly overjoyed and blessed out of my socks.

I didn't know it but I had experienced the truth of God's word. John 10:10 "I have come that they may have life, and that they may have it more abundantly."

Matthew16:25 "For whoever desires to save his life will lose it, but whoever loses his life for My sake will find it." I had found life and it was wonderful.

I thought back to previous holidays, sitting in front of the T.V. for hours on end switching channels as quickly as I could, as one programme finished on one channel and the other about to start on another of the two existing channels! The difference between existing and living was incredible. There was no bigger buzz than serving God and following Jesus.

The next summer holiday saw me go to an Inner City Outreach in Coventry for a week. I do not remember who organised it or how I ended up going but I knew God set me up for another adventure. I went on my own not knowing a soul: the story of my life. I met people from all over England. We had Bible teaching from Eric Delve and prayer in the morning and then preparation for the afternoon outreach. I discovered that this 'Fishing' had a different slant on things.

I was placed in the drama group. We did a sketch on the street outside the big main store in the town centre. We had to cause a commotion to gather a crowd. Then someone would tell their testimony in about five minutes flat. The drama people, including shy me, started clucking like hens and flapping our arms like wings, running in and out and around each other causing a lot of noise and interest.

People gathered and asked what was going on. Some of the team were in place as an audience already.

Someone in the team asked us what we were doing.

"We are chickens."

"What makes you think you are chickens?"

"We live in a henhouse and eat corn."

Sorry you are not chickens.

Next we changed into aeroplanes and we quickly revved up the sound of engines and zoomed around. We were asked once more what we thought we were.

We replied in unison that we were aeroplanes.

What made us think that?

"We live in a hangar and use fuel."

"Sorry, no you are not."

Next we walked around with clasped hands singing amen.

What were we supposed to be now?

"We are Christians."

"How do you know?"

"We go to church and sing hymns."

"Sorry that does not make you a Christian."

We all asked, "So what is a Christian?"

At that point a really strong-voiced team member leaped forward from the crowd and explained what a Christian is and how you become a Christian.

After he finished we all mingled with the crowd asking them what they thought. I saw for the first time as mad and as daft and as strange as I felt doing the drama, it was a crowd puller and it did lead to great conversations. We invited the people to come to the church for the evening meeting. Many actually came, much to my surprise and delight!

After round one was over we repeated the sketch again till it was time to go back. We learned quite a few crowd-pulling sketches. Each of us had to also give testimony after the drama at some point during the week.

It was while in Coventry that I experienced fasting for the first time - drinking only water for a day and in place of eating, praying in our groups. Talk about challenged! However, I actually fasted for a full day and at one minute past midnight stood in a long queue at the nearby chip shop!

The praise and worship at the start of the evening meeting was spectacular. All the songs were completely new to me and they touched me deeply. Oh for some in our church back home. I did not understand then the difference between religion and relationship with Jesus. But I had tasted Jesus and I loved Him.

A friend at church was invited to a meeting in a school which a colleague's church was having. I agreed to go with him. I was shocked to hear the minister of The King's Church in Motherwell walk on the platform in Coltness High School and say, "God wants to say something different from what I have prepared. So praise, worship and testify till I hear what His message is." Then he walked off the stage!

We sang, praised, worshipped and listened to testimonies for nearly an hour!

I could never imagine that happening in my church! Holy Spirit versus religion was seen again.

Finally the pastor came back to tell everyone God wanted to speak about healing. So the pastor shared some Bible stories of healings and then asked if anyone needed healing.

I had suffered periodically for two or three years with a skin condition. My face would swell really badly so that one eye was closed. I had a painful, red itchy rash on my face, neck, ear and hands. The rash would weep then turn into scabs and then became very dry with the skin falling off like snowflakes. The whole process would take five weeks before it cleared up.

It had just started again on my hands and face that week. As I sat in that secondary school, my face and hands were sore, red, and itchy and felt as if they were on fire.

What would happen if I went forward for prayer? Prayer couldn't kill me, could it? Our church had never asked for people to come forward for prayer before. I did not know that Hebrews 13:8 says, "Jesus Christ is the same yesterday, today, and forever."

I did not know that what Jesus did in my Bible He still does today. However, I was about to find out!

As shy as I used to be, and forcing myself, I walked forward in front of the hundreds of people. My need was greater than my fear! I simply reasoned that if prayer could help this dreadful skin condition then I would take it even if it meant standing up in front of all these people!

I was the only person up at the front of the auditorium. I did not feel at all comfortable knowing everyone was watching me! As I perspired with tension, my face was more painfully on fire.

The pastor walked forward and asked me what the problem was. Actually he could see it, so he called over two men in suits, who put their hands on my head and shoulders. They prayed in a foreign language and asked me to sit on a seat in the front row. As they prayed I felt an incredible heat from the top of my head to the soles of my feet. All I could think about was if I continued to sweat like that my deodorant wouldn't work!

The next thing I remembered was opening my eyes and seeing loads of people standing in front of me and sitting all around me.

An old lady was testifying how God had healed her arthritic knee. She stood on the stage and showed everyone how she could bend her knee easily with no pain. Her son also testified to his mother being healed as she could not bend her knee at all before she got prayer, because a metal pin had been inserted to keep her knee straight! (I saw this lady testify in a church in Motherwell a week later showing everyone an x-ray proving her pin had moved four centimetres enabling her knee to bend with no sign of arthritis.)

I had been unaware of what had been going on for half an hour and had not seen or heard anything. I was completely at peace. It was a wonderful feeling. I didn't understand about the power of the Holy Spirit or speaking in tongues or healing. I was awestruck! I thoroughly enjoyed hearing and seeing the number of people who were now healed.

When I went back to my seat, there was an ice cold fan blowing on my face and hands. It took the heat and pain and itch away. It was great. I commented on what a great idea of putting on that fan to cool the red itchy rash on my neck and face. Where was it? I could not see it! No one had a clue what I was talking about; from what they were saying there was no fan and yes the place was extremely hot!

Next morning I got up as usual to discover my skin condition had completely gone. I have never experienced it since. This was my first healing.

I met a new friend, Evie, from The King's Church in Motherwell and she would invite me to special meetings. I thoroughly enjoyed going to these meetings as I recognised her church was different from mine.

We used to pray together. I admit I was ignorant about prayer but I was hungry and wanted to learn. She had an annoying habit. As soon as I started to pray she would mutter under her breath. I honestly thought it was really rude of her! One night however, I could not tolerate it one minute longer, so I told her I thought she was being rude talking while I was trying to pray. She went on to explain she meant no harm by it, but that in actual fact, she was praying in the Spirit. Oh the foreign language I had heard!

She went on to explain about baptism in the Holy Spirit. I thought it weird and just decided to leave it alone. I still did not understand.

I had a Roman Catholic friend I had met through Brownies. She and her husband asked me to a Charismatic meeting in Glasgow. I did not know what that was. I learned it emphasized a personal relationship with Jesus and using the gifts of the Holy Spirit. The place was filled to capacity. I found out that a very petite Irish nun was the speaker; she was indeed petite.

The meeting started with songs; I hardly knew any of them, then out of nowhere I lost my place in the song booklet. Everyone started to sing beautiful strange words and the sound seemed to rise higher and higher. It actually sounded wonderful but weird. All of a sudden without anyone leading, this strange singing stopped all at the same time. The nun spoke then prayed for all the priests who had come from all over to hear her. They lined up like rows of sardines. She went along the front row praying for the Holy Spirit to touch them. One by one they fell back on the floor, lying as if dead! What was she doing to them? Killing them?

My friend's husband told me not to panic as they were being 'slain in the Spirit'.

Help! I was right. She was killing them.

I started to bolt out of my balcony seat. They encouraged me to stay. It was my first experience of seeing how the Holy Spirit comes upon a person and as they are overcome by His presence, they fall to the ground. Another learning curve! Just because a thing is unfamiliar does not make it wrong!

Not long after this, I was invited to an outreach meeting by The King's Church, in Coatbridge High School. I took a car load of the Bible Class with me. We sat up at the back of the assembly hall. The praise and worship was great and one could have listened to the guest speaker all night.

A young couple brought their baby in late. They sat in front of us. I could not help think they should have had the baby at home and not brought it out so late to a meeting. There I go again with my own opinions and thoughts.

I was utterly amazed listening to the speaker's testimony of what God had done in his life.

Even though it was years ago I still remember how God used the speaker's friend to pray for him to be healed of arthritis and get out of his wheelchair. The fingers of one hand were not healed of their sloping because God wanted him to remember how he had been touched.

Mike Pusey, the speaker, told a story of how God took him to a Polynesian island. He believed that God had said the whole village would be saved. However, when he spoke to the chief he was not given permission to share the gospel with the villagers. He was disappointed. He prayed for God to intervene. When he heard that the fishing had been really bad of late, he felt God say to go to the chief and ask him if he could pray for fish to be caught. No fish meant no food.

So he obediently went again to the chief and asked him if he could pray for the fishermen to get a good catch of fish. The chief allowed him to pray.

Early next morning the speaker was awoken by a great commotion all around where he was staying as people ran shouting on their way to the beach. He followed.

When he arrived at the beach he could not believe his eyes. There on the beach lay three rows of huge tuna fish, lying fin to fin, along the seven miles of golden sand. They were lying in three straight lines. He and the villagers were all utterly amazed.

The chief thanked him for his prayer and gave him permission to share the gospel with the whole village. He said each person gave their heart to Jesus.

As I sat and listened I yearned for such stories to be part of my life. I knew God could do anything and I so wanted Him to do it through me. I realised I was actually jealous of his testimony.

At the end we watched people run up the aisles to give their lives to Jesus. Why did we not see that in our church?

After the call for salvation, he asked if anyone wanted to be filled with the Holy Spirit. Again people flocked to the front including some my Bible Class members who slowly walked forward for prayer. They came back speaking in tongues, their faces glowing.

What on earth will their parents say? Oh dear I am for it! These thoughts plagued my mind. The woman, who had prayed for one of the girls, followed her up the aisle to where I was sitting. She took one look at me and told me not to fear and asked if I too would like to receive the baptism of the Holy Spirit. She said after I had prayed and nothing happened that she saw I was terrified. She explained that the gift was what God wanted for me to receive by faith and that God is a God of love.

She prayed for the fear to go and encouraged me to open my mouth to be willing to receive the heavenly prayer language. Immediately I opened my mouth and moved my tongue, I spoke odd words. I must admit it felt strange and I thought I must be making it up! But I knew I was speaking in tongues!

I experienced a joy filling me like none other.

After praying for people to be filled with the Spirit, the speaker then asked if anyone had need of healing. I sat interested. I knew God could heal.

The young couple with the baby sitting in front of us, jumped up and ran to the front. The speaker said that we should all stretch out our hands and pray because the baby was born without eyes.

Everyone stretched out their hands and prayed in tongues. It looked like they were making a Heil Hitler sign. I had never seen people do this before. Seemingly their raised hands meant they were agreeing with the speaker's prayers.

The baby began to scream. I thought it was terrible getting people to do this as it must be hurting the baby somehow.

I was wrong again. The couple brought the baby back with two new wet eyes, where before there were none! Glory to God with whom all things are possible!

Is He not Creator God after all?

We all went home that night singing in the Spirit. When we stopped at the traffic lights, we looked across at the car next to us. The occupants were giving us queer looks! I cannot imagine why!

There was such a hunger in me for the things of God. I met so many ordinary people with extraordinary stories of how they met Jesus. I heard how Jesus had changed their lives and how God had jobs for them to do. I met one man who said that Jesus turned his alcohol into furniture! He was saved, gave up drinking alcohol and bought furniture with his money instead.

I asked people everywhere how they had met Jesus. I met many who said they had a private faith and it was not for sharing. At the time I thought that this faith was not a Bible faith!

I bought books by the hundreds in my thirst for more of God. I read about villages, cities, jungles, peoples all being touched by the power of God and the truth of His Word. I read about signs, wonders and miracles taking place when people prayed and God answered. The only problem was I wished it would happen to me!

Moving to Scripture Union in Perth

It got to Hogmanay 1985, the last day of the year. It was after the bells at midnight and up in my attic bedroom I felt somehow I was playing games with God. I had been saved for three years and I was so hungry and desperate to really know God more and please Him.

I found myself on the floor, prostrate before my Father in Heaven, groaning and crying.

About 2 a.m. I cried out, "Here I am Lord, do whatever you want with my life."

"Leave teaching," was the prompt reply!

How could I? I loved teaching and anyway what else could I do except perhaps clean houses?

I love the way God speaks and also how He moves.

At that time I was taking my Bible Class to Glenrothes for youth weekends to a Church of Scotland that my friends Trevor and Mairi attended. We would join their group for games, Bible Teaching and praise and prayer.

We had amazing times. Their minister asked me if I had ever thought of becoming a deaconess. That led me to investigate the process of becoming a Church of Scotland deaconess. I even went to the Church of Scotland headquarters at 121 George Street in Edinburgh on a course to find out more about it. I was rejected. Thank you Lord, You always know best!

It was not the way or will of God for my life but I was trying my best to make something happen.

I was soon to learn; God closes doors in your nose!

Nothing was happening and nine months later David Geddes, a Scripture Union staff worker, visited my Scripture Union group at school in Clarkston Airdrie. It was he who gave me my first rebuke in love.

Basically he said if God was saying 'No', there would be no 'Go'! I didn't like to hear what he said but I knew it was the truth that I needed to hear.

I prayed again that night, "God will You make it clear? I am willing to do anything but don't know what You want me to do!" I learned how to let go and let God!

The next day I got a phone call after school from the head of Schools at Scripture Union in Glasgow. She invited me to Glasgow to see her and tell me about a job going in Scripture Union Tayside.

My headmaster took my class and gave me an afternoon off so that this woman could tell me all about the job in Tayside and what it would entail. To be honest I did not really hear her. I was amazed at how messy her little office was. There were piles of books, folders and papers stacked untidily everywhere. How could she work in this mess?

It was decided that I should have an application form which I could take away and complete. I duly took it home and had a quick read over the questions and realised I did not know any of the answers. The only part of the application form I could readily fill in were the personal questions at the end. I really wasn't thinking about a job in Tayside! What would my father do if I left home because then there would no one to help with his old paralysed aunt who stayed with us.

One Sunday night a few weeks later, my Bible Class and Youth Fellowship went to an evening in Bellshill

Y.M.C.A. A gospel group from Perth called 'Gravel and Boulders,' later to become 'The Bottom Line,' were playing and doing their usual 'God slot' talk. At the end, Brian Souter, one of the band came up and said there was a job going in Scripture Union in Tayside. I should consider applying.

You know God really does make His ways known. Isaiah 30:21 says "Your ears shall hear a word behind you, saying, "This is the way, walk in it, whenever you turn to the right hand or whenever you turn to the left."

I delivered the teenagers home, returned the community bus, came in and read the application form more carefully this time. It was after midnight.

"Who is the person of the Holy Spirit and what is His work?"

It was full of questions I didn't really know how to answer. It would take days of research before I could answer them.

I remember Hezekiah spread a letter out before the Lord and prayed, in 2 Kings 19:14. So that was what I did!

I slapped my hand on top of the application form and prayed, "Lord if You want me to get this job, You are going to have to fill in this application form and answer all these questions."

I got up and took my pen, opened the application form and was amazed as my pen flew over the paper writing answers I did not know! I was reading and learning as I wrote. It was amazing! I did not even check for grammar or spelling errors, a thing I would normally do. After all it was very late and I had school next day. I put it in an envelope, addressed it and left it beside the kitchen phone, telling myself that if I felt to post it when I got up in the morning, then I would.

Let me tell you again God moves supernaturally, very naturally.

My father came in from work at 2.30 a.m. and decided to do his invoices before going to bed that night. He had never done that before! When I came downstairs in the morning he told me that he had stuck a stamp on my letter and posted it along with his mail at 4 a.m. at the head post office box in Motherwell, about four miles away, as he wanted his mail to catch the earliest post!

God saw to it that His will was being done. My hesitancy didn't stop Him.

I was invited to an interview in Perth for the job of schools staff worker in Tayside.

At the interview I heard God speak through me and give answers I did not know. The job was mine not because man decided but because God's plans were being worked out. My father knew before I did that I got the job as God told him the job was mine. He was not a Christian.

As a Bible Class we went to Arbroath Baptist Centre for my last Bible class holiday before I left for Perth. It was out of this world. They asked me for permission to allow them to give me a surprise farewell or a nice send off! One I would always remember! I said, "Yes!"

Before we left one of the leaders said to bring some old clothes I would be able to put in the bin after my farewell! No further clues were given!

At the end of this holiday the teenagers gave me five minutes warning. They planned a unique send off. "Plug your ears and nostrils!" one of the leaders advised.

I rather foolishly agreed that they could do anything but I must have use of my hands.

They tied me to the clothes pole in the garden at the back of the Arbroath Baptist Centre but they left my arms free. I was, of course, wearing my old clothes. Each teenager had thought of, collected, or bought something for me to always remember!

An orderly line of teenagers stood in front of me smiling, one being a photographer. First of all one of them poured a tin of pink emulsion paint over my head; a basin of sand followed, and then burst teabags and even a plastic carrier bag full of seaweed. All this was followed by cold leftover mince and even toast crusts! The one item, however, which nearly killed me, was dry custard powder. As it was thrown, I happened to open my mouth. Bull's eye! My open mouth was full of the dry yellow substance which went down my throat, dried my mouth and made me nearly sick.

But seeing they were a very kindly group, they gave me some water, waited till I had composed myself then continued with their send off!

They had even thoughtfully turned on the shower, gave me a nice clean towel and left me to shower for a very long time. I can tell you I was washing tea and sand out of my hair and ears for days afterwards.

It was really hard saying goodbye to what had been a really special time in my life. The story of Abraham spoke volumes. He had to leave his family and take a journey to a destination that only God knew about. There is pain in leaving but comfort in the knowledge that God has a plan and a purpose and a place and a people for us to connect with and enjoy for His glory. He also goes with us.

It was simply God's will that I move on through the door He had opened.

God works all things together for our good when we simply yield to Him. I struggled for months trying to make a way for me to get a deaconesses job with the Church of Scotland and for nine months nothing happened. I yielded to God with the Scripture Union job and behold, I was moving to Perth in the twinkling of an eye!

Elizebeth, one of the Bible Class girls, who was unemployed at the time, volunteered to help look after my dad's old aunt. My dad's sister helped too. God had provided help for my father. I could go to Perth knowing he was not on his own. (My father's old aunt died weeks after I started my new job in Perth.)

I was astonished at the provision of my Father in Heaven. He knew what I needed before I did!

Almost immediately, I was offered a tenement flat with two weeks free rent. A friend and my cousin's husband stayed in the flat and painted it beautifully all ready for me to move into. Over a couple of weeks, friends and family gave me a coffee table, three piece suite, curtains, carpets, a cooker, a fridge, a living room cabinet and a kitchen table and two benches as well as towels, crockery and cutlery. To come from diverse people and places was super but to see it all in one place and matching was incredible! Simply put, God the Creator was my interior designer!

Before my suite and other furniture arrived, I had a bean bag to sit on and a small black and white T.V. One night while watching the news about a famine in Ethiopia, I had a unique experience. I felt as if I was one of the children who was starving. I ached and felt weak and started to cry as I prayed for the famine sufferers. Suddenly I felt God literally lift me onto His knee and hold me. Comfort and peace flooded me.

I have never forgotten sitting on God's knee and His arms holding me. He is, after all, my Abba Daddy.

I settled quickly into my new life in Perth. I did not feel strange or lonely at all. I loved my new job.

Initially one of the more mature SU school workers, Esme Duncan, took me under her wing and showed me the ropes of Scripture Union. She was excellent as I shadowed her in Aberdeen.

It was soon time for me to get on with the SU job in Tayside.

I went to the Nazarene Church in Perth for that first year.

I used to think, in my ignorance, that the Church of Scotland was the church in Scotland. I had mainly frequented Church of Scotland events, except the King's Church in Motherwell of course. In my ignorance I believed, for example, that Baptists were a cult!

I had so much to learn as I rubbed shoulders with wonderful colleagues, mature in the faith, sound in the Word of God, and experienced in obeying God's voice and will.

Very quickly I had the feeling that I had been with Scripture Union for years and that Perth was my home. I loved life in Perth.

I remember one of the first cards I received was from a Dundee Church of Scotland deaconess. I will never forget the truth and admonition it contained. She drew a picture of a car with Jesus in the driving seat, leading and guiding as Lord. I was in the back seat being taken, not directing. That card and drawing were powerful and, though simple, spoke volumes!

Whatever I did, I allowed Jesus to lead because I was His follower after all.

As the Scripture Union Schools Staff worker in Tayside (what a mouthful), I visited Scripture Union groups in primary and secondary schools, took assemblies, helped with Scripture Union camps, promoted the camps, spoke at churches and youth groups, attended prayer meetings and travelled for hundreds of miles. It should be noted that I slept in my own flat for only three months that first year!

What a fun time I had meeting all the lovely SU family and friends and getting out and about in lovely scenery. I saw the cleanest cows ever and the earth was rich, red and fertile. It was wonderful. I discovered there is life outside of school. God's creation was truly amazing. I was so blessed.

Talk about never being bored! Life was full and abundant just as Jesus promised. I was thrilled to know that I was the vessel and Jesus was leading and the Holy Spirit moved through me.

It has also to be said that I truly felt out of my depth all the time! At one prayer meeting I suggested that if we prayed in pairs more prayers could be prayed and so answered. Talk about a revelation, or a revolution! The local minister was there that night and he did not like it at all. So it was normal prayers after that, one at a time. It seemed alien to some people that God could hear more than one prayer at a time or that there could possibly be a new way of doing things.

I remember having to go to a school in Breadalbane just after I came to SU. The headmistress asked me, "Do you sing!"

Absolutely not!

"Do you play the guitar?"

Sorry to disappoint!

"Well what can you do then?"

"Quake in my shoes and pray hard" I replied internally!

What had happened was, Ian White, the famous Christian singer and songwriter was in the job before me. Everyone knows how talented he is; as he sang his way around all the schools.

I could not fill his shoes for I was to walk in my own God-shaped and God-created shoes. So instead of singing I told Bible stories and used drama with the children to make it come alive. Although I could not sing, I did anyway!

God said in Psalm 139:14 that I am fearfully and wonderfully made and in Ephesians 2:10 I am to do and enjoy the beforehand prepared works He had fashioned for me, May Dow!

I was just me! I could not be anyone else but I was to allow Jesus to live through me.

Scripture Union days were not all plain sailing. When you yield to God there is joy but also pain. I remember one time being asked to speak on 'Prayer' at a meeting for students in Dundee. Every time I started to prepare or tried to continue to prepare 'Prayer' I kept hearing "This is not My will for these students." What a struggle I had!

Travelling to the meeting that day as I crossed the River Tay, I heard the Holy Spirit say,

"Will you put aside your notes and let Me minister and speak?"

At that time I did not really understand what that entailed.

How could I disregard their request and say, 'No talk on prayer today?'

I did not fully appreciate that in fulfilling their request, I was actually saying NO TO GOD!

I got to the meeting, was introduced and it was stated I would be speaking on 'Prayer'. I started to speak on prayer. It was flat and 'as dead as a dodo' but more importantly I knew I was disobeying God. So I stopped speaking, repented and told them what the Holy Spirit had said as I drove across the River Tay. I waited. They were open to a change of plan. But if prayer was off the agenda, what was on it?

Baptism in the Holy Spirit!

I had no notes, nothing prepared. What was I to do?

Simply put, yield myself to the Holy Spirit. Up until that time I had never experienced anything like it.

I heard myself go from Scripture to Scripture letting Him fill my mouth with His truth. The amazing thing was that the words did not even come into my mind first. It was an amazing experience to be a vessel for God to use; when I became available He enabled!

I was unprepared, yes, but I was available and God spoke fluently. It was after all, His Word! Many were baptised in the Holy Spirit speaking with tongues. It was wonderful!

BUT!

At the end, a minister's daughter ran out the room crying. She locked herself in the toilet and let's just say, I had another first-hand experience of 'suffering for the sake of Christ.'

Letters of complaint went to my boss, and a little chat was in order! Answers failed me. However, I knew I had been obedient to God and if this was counting the cost so be it! It would not be the last time!

God knows everything so I learned to hand it all over to Him.

It was clear, very clear, not everyone likes the way God moves by His Holy Spirit. Religion hates the Holy Spirit and gets very upset when He moves. I was learning all the time. Sometimes painfully!

While in SU in Perth I clashed badly with one particular person. We tended to grate on each other's nerves. I felt intimidated and unhappy living in disunity with him. God commands blessing where there is unity. However, it's not fun when we have a 'problem' with someone. Things got so bad that I could barely look at him. My heart became hard and it was a horrible time. It went on for months. There was a Scripture Union camp on and I ended up sharing a box room with my boss. She saw there was something up. It's sad when we have problems; they show up on our countenance because our joy goes out the window!

I shared my problem with her and she listened carefully to my side of the story. She reminded me that there is always another side to a story and God knows both sides perfectly.

She shared a truth I have never forgotten. Simply put: God loved my 'temporary enemy' or my 'frenemy', as much as He loved me, as much as He loved Jesus.

"How could God love him?" I thought. Then just as quickly, "How could God love me?"

How, really doesn't matter so much, as He does!

"You need to forgive him and love him," she informed me again! There's that word again. Forgive. Forgive. Forgive. Remember it's an act of my will, not just a feeling.

I drove sixty four miles home, crying to God, releasing my problem person or my 'frenemy' to my forgiveness. I was exhausted but was smiling.

The test was the next night. There was a meeting on and he would be there. Truth was, he had not changed one iota, but I most certainly had. When I looked at him, I genuinely loved him with the love of God. He did not irritate me in the slightest as he had done previously.

Peter, the S.U. Bookshop manager, came up to me at the end of the night and informed me, "Something has happened to you. You don't react to him like you did." I quickly shared my weekend experience. God is so good and His ways always work. I had passed the test and learned and applied the lesson.

While I was at the Nazarene church during my first year in Perth, the minister intimated that there would be a baptismal service in the River Tay for adult believers.

Now I had been through an adult baptism service in the church back home and so ignored what was being said. However you cannot ignore something when God highlights it. My daily reading was about water baptism: Jesus being baptised by John in the River Jordan. He simply said if you are following Me then do as I do. If I went through the waters of baptism, I want you to do likewise.

What did I do? I prayed for confirmation of course. Will we ever come to a place where we so know the voice of the Holy Spirit that we obey Him immediately without the need to have it confirmed a hundred times?

On the following Sunday evening, one of the 'Training for Freedom' prisoners from Perth jail who went to the church, popped in to see me on his way back to prison. My flat was opposite the prison. If he had too much time before he needed to go back, then he would pop in for a coffee and a prayer.

He stood at the door and said he had a word from God for me.

"God wants you baptised in water." Acts 2:38 Then Peter said to them, "Repent, and let everyone of you be baptized in the name of Jesus Christ for the remission of sins; and you shall receive the gift of the Holy Spirit."

Then he left.

So I attended the baptism classes. I understood the significance of full immersion in water. It signifies the death, burial and resurrection of Jesus. There was no getting away from what God was saying. But I had a major problem causing me grave concern. I was petrified of going under the water and the water going up my nose and in my ears! To me it was a huge deal. On the morning of the baptism I woke up to hear, "I went to the cross for you and you are scared of getting your face wet for Me." "Well when you put it that way Lord! Help me be obedient to Your word."

That morning was overcast and wet. In the afternoon, we went to Moncrieff Island where everyone had gathered. I prayed to enjoy the experience rather than be petrified. My turn came. I waded into the cold water. It was September. The sun peeked through the clouds as I heard the minister ask me, "Do you believe in the Lord Jesus Christ as your personal Lord and Saviour?"

"I do" was my reply.

"Then I baptise you in the name of the Father, the Son and the Holy Spirit" and down under the water I went. It was incredible. I actually opened my eyes to see a circle of sunlight on the surface of the water.

I heard an audible voice say, "This is my beloved daughter, May, in whom I am well pleased."

That time under the water seemed to last for ages although I know it was only a fleeting moment. It was another wonderful experience I am so glad I did not miss!

Unfortunately not everyone was pleased with my obedience to Scripture. My former minister spoke to me as he had heard what I had done a few weeks previously. He told me he would need to remove my name from the Church of Scotland roll because of what I had done, as they don't believe in adult water baptism. The peace of God flooded me and I simply stated that as long as my name was written in the Lamb's Book of Life in heaven I would be fine.

When I accompanied a youth group to Iona, BJ, the bus driver was full of questions. He heard the gospel and it disturbed him. God would not send good people to hell, would He? How often has that question been mulled over by the millions? He could not find peace and appeared a few weeks later on my doorstep. On opening the door, his finger inches from my nose, his initial greeting was "Hello. I have a bone to pick with you!"

Brian came in, with all his questions. The gospel is called Good News but it does contain bad news too. Weeks went by till he finally came to a place that he knew he was a sinner and repented of his sins. Going away that night, he stood at his car door and asked, "What can God do with me? I am just a bus driver. I was a dunce at school. I can't do anything for God."

God has a plan for every one of us. The plans vary in each person's case, but the fact is He, the Living God, wants to use us for His purposes to bless the world. It does not matter whether we are rich or poor, intelligent or not, God has a plan for everyone's life.

A few weeks following his conversion, Brian was asked to drive a double decker bus to Romania. His boss said that a woman from Fife, Nan Beveridge, was taking aid and a driver was required. He was offered the job. It was a journey driving through many countries. They saw the hand of God help them by providing help at the borders, getting fuel and many times having someone to show them exactly where they were supposed to go. He took aid many times, usually spending two weeks in Romania followed by two weeks at home.

However, one specific time would change his life forever.

This particular time they visited a new orphanage. Many children were abandoned at birth as Nicolae Ceausescu, the former president of Romania, had banned contraception and abortion in an attempt to increase the population. The parents, however, could not afford their children and abandoned them. The children were assessed and put in different orphanages depending on their abilities or disabilities.

The team from Scotland were shown round this new orphanage by the deputy director. When they came to look in one particular room, a small eight year old boy ran, flew through the air wrapping his sticky fingers round the bus driver's neck. The youngster kept repeating, "Tata! Tata!" Brian later learned that this meant, "Daddy! Daddy!"

Out of the many children he had seen over these trips, there was something special about this one. During the time there, the little boy, shadowed the bus driver whenever possible. They became close. Language was a problem. Love is never a problem.

This small boy had been in another orphanage and one day some time previously had been summoned to the Director's office. He was informed he was going to be moved to another orphanage. He did not want to go and leave his friends. However, he was informed it was not an option. He would be moving. The Director was surprised to hear the young boy declare, "A foreign man will come to be my father!"

The boy was now in this orphanage in Ineu, which was a 700 year old Turkish fortress. It housed 600 boys aged 8 to 18 years.

Over the years Brian took aid many times to this orphanage. On one trip permission was given to take the boy and some of his friends on an outing. A rare event! Brian developed a genuine love for the young boy and felt he had to do something for him. He came to the place that he was willing to give up his life in Scotland and was even prepared to live in Romania if God so willed.

Brian decided to take a year off work, move to Romania, rent a cottage and do voluntary work in the orphanage. Permission was given for his little companion to live with him so many nights a week.

During his year off, the little boy and Brian did odd jobs together. He taught him some English words. They were like father and son. Truly, Brian was Tata!

When praying he felt God wanted him to adopt the boy and bring him to Scotland. Imagine a son without having a wife. An answer to prayer!

So started the long process of adopting the boy. It took many hours of reading and understanding all the information given to him, never mind the mountain of paperwork both from Romania and the UK that had to be filled in. Obtaining visas and a passport were fun. Not!

The day before he was due to drive to Romania to bring his soon to be adopted son home to Scotland, he was watching the TV. A Grampian 'God slot' programme was on and the minister was telling a story. In it he shared how a man was walking along a beach when he noticed a small boy in the distance bend down, pick something up from the sand and place it gently in the sea. As he got up closer, he saw hundreds of starfish. The man asked the boy, "What are you doing?" The little boy said that he was putting the star fish in the water. "If I don't, the sun will come up and dry them out before the tide comes in." The man told him, "You can't save them all!" The small boy picked up a starfish in the palm of his hand and gently placing it in the sea said, "This one is safe!"

God was speaking very clearly. Brian, the bus driver, knew he could not make a difference to the six hundred orphans in the orphanage in Romania but he also knew that he could do it for one and make him safe. It took the bus driver eight years to get the boy home.

Finally his son Eion arrived in his new home in Spittalfield, near Perth, in 1999. When asked about his life, he would say, "My life began when I came here!"

This story blessed and challenged me. According to academic standards he may have been a dunce at school, but this new father excelled in persistence, diligence and sacrificial giving in the fulfilling of God's plan for his ordinary life and being a blessing to his new son.

One event where I showed no persistence and was refusing God's plan for my life, was when I was asked to take part in a mission in Edinburgh University. It was way out of my league.

I actually did a Jonah and ran fast! I knew a basic, simple gospel and felt I would be totally inadequate to take part in debates, question times in pubs and such things with all those students. Children, primary age, were more my league. I was actually filled with intense fear and dread.

I became ill with gall bladder trouble. I was not making it up! The pain was horrendous and at times I could not even move or breathe. The doctor said my gallbladder was inflamed.

Oh a genuinely good reason to miss the mission in Edinburgh! I would not be lying. I had a genuine get out clause!

When I phoned to inform the organisers, they said, "We'll pray and by next week you'll be absolutely fine." Believe it or not, that was not music to my ears. Yes, you have guessed it, by the Sunday I was fine. After church I discovered I had a puncture. Great! I could not go! But it was no problem to the guys in the church. They had fixed it before I could call off from going to the mission. I so wanted to 'do a Jonah' and run in the opposite direction!

As I sat in my now fixed car I prayed through gritted teeth, "OK God, I will go to Edinburgh on mission but You had better do it for I'm way out of my depth!" I drove to Edinburgh speaking in tongues, or roaring actually!

Did you know it's a pretty uncomfortable and terrifying feeling getting out of the boat? After all it looks like we will sink in the water!

The first night of the mission I went to bed praying hard. I had a significant dream; my first God dream.

In the dream I knew I was running along a very dark tunnel with many doors on each side. There was a light away at the far end. I was running for my life. I was petrified but I did not know what I was running from. Whatever was chasing me was snapping at me, just missing my heels. It was about to catch me.

Terrified I would be caught by whatever it was, but also curious to know what was actually chasing me, I quickly looked behind me. I was shocked and horrified to find the ugliest thing ever! It was a huge head with a horrible, ugly face covered in long dirty matted hair, with cruel eyes, a wide mouth filled with long, sharp, curved teeth. I knew it hated me and what was more wanted to kill me!

Racing faster than ever towards the light, fear filling my pulsating heart, a voice from Scripture suddenly filled my mind. "He who is in you is greater than what is in that thing chasing you!" (1 John 4:4.) It was as if I was a cartoon character putting the brakes on, digging my heels into the floor, stopping myself dead!

I turned round quickly and said or rather started to say, "JESUS" when the thing screamed shrilly, "Oh don't say that name. I beg you don't say that name!" I could see the thing was petrified of the name of Jesus and quaked in its footless body. I could feel its absolute fear at the name of Jesus. I also saw its reaction when I started to say the name of Jesus. It was as if the name of Jesus caused it great distress and pain and torment. It was wonderful to watch the power of the name of Jesus at work! It was really awesome!

Great strength and more courage welled up from the depths of my being, chasing any remaining fear away. Taking great delight, all fear having been completely dispelled, I stated loudly with intense joy and a holy boldness that victory statement, "In Jesus' Name." I had not finished when the demon shrivelled and shrieked, "Don't say that name please!" Polite demon or not, I shouted loudly "Jesus." "JESUS," I proclaimed boldly again, knowing it was tortured by the name that is above every other name. It screamed painfully, contorting in agony at hearing the name of Jesus and then finally exploded into nothing!

Great joy and relief flooded me and I knew but I knew, Jesus in me was tremendously powerful and that the demons of hell were petrified of the name of Jesus. I had just witnessed this truth. I needed to know this truth before the next day because He knew what lay ahead of me!

JESUS

On the second day of the mission I met Claire, a student who had a Christian friend who was not doing too well and she asked if I could pray for her.

So we went back to her student residence. Basically she had gone up Calton Hill, had witnessed cloaked and hooded people in a circle chanting. She hid. One came over to her and spoke over her. She was petrified and ran for her life. Since that night, as a Christian, she had tremendous difficulty reading her Bible and praying.

What were we to do? Pray of course, asking God to do what was necessary to bring a change.

As we started to pray, she shot into the corner of her bed, rolling herself into a tight ball. I explained about the baptism in the Spirit and she prayed and received. Literally the Holy Spirit led us in prayer for her. We cut her off from the evil and prayed for her to be blessed and filled with peace, love and joy. She was filled indeed! This was the first time I had prayed for someone to be set free or delivered. I had not a clue but once again allowed the Holy Spirit to fill my mouth.

After praying for her we walked along the corridor outside her room. We passed an open door on the right and I asked whose room this was as I felt an evil presence. I was informed it was the janitor's room. The janitor, a lady, wasn't in so I stepped quickly into the room and prayed the blood of Jesus over it and her. It turned out that the janitor was a practising witch, who weeks later left her job!

Talk about another learning curve. The whole week at Edinburgh University was an opportunity to experience God connecting me with His 'whosoever' I was destined to meet at that time. It was an incredible experience I would not have wanted to miss. I saw students saved and baptised in the Spirit and delivered. It was a lesson in yielding to God even though fear and trepidation tried to make me back out and run away. The devil will try anything to put us off course. When we fail to press through into the victory Jesus gives us, we miss God's plan for our lives and allow ourselves to be robbed of giving God glory. It also robs those, whom we are destined to meet, of encountering Jesus in and through us.

God is so good. He knows all about everything and everyone and our part in His plans.

It's OK to feel the fear, lean on Him and be obedient anyway. Easy to say but it takes determination and grit and the right choice to press through into victory! It is a battle. But we need to remember we have the victory.

Working for Scripture Union was a privilege and I thoroughly enjoyed my job. The lessons I learned I passed on to the people I met. An SU camp cook phoned me one Friday night in a terrible state. She had had another fight with her teenage son. He had changed, becoming oppressed, moody, isolated and argumentative. He spent hours in his room interested in occult things and listening to his dark music. He had stormed out saying he was going to stay with his father for the weekend.

Sharing with her the power of the blood of Jesus, I encouraged her to go into his room and pray the blood of Jesus over everything, which she did.

On Sunday night, her son returned, grunted to his mum as he went up the stairs to his room.

In a flash he rushed downstairs, came into the living room and grabbed her shoulders and shook her demanding to know what she had done to his room. Shocked at the speed of events which had interrupted her quiet Sunday evening, she simply said that she had dusted his room on the Friday after he had left. She had completely forgotten about praying in it.

"You have done something to my room. It doesn't even feel the same!" he stated angrily. "I cannot stay here. I am going to live with my dad!"

As Christians we fail to utilise the weapons of our warfare which are mighty to the pulling down of strongholds as the Bible says in Ephesians 6:10-12, "Finally, my brethren, be strong in the Lord and in the strength of His might. Put on the whole armour of God, that you may be able to stand against the wiles of the devil. For we do not wrestle against flesh and blood, but against the principalities, against powers, against the rulers of the darkness of this age, against spiritual hosts of wickedness in the heavenly places."

God can teach us how to defeat Satan when we need to.

One such learning curve was while I was away at a children's camp. Coming up the driveway to the old mansion, I heard the Holy Spirit say that I was to pray in every room. So the first thing I did was to get out of the car and go and pray in every room. Another leader arrived just as I was starting. She and I had gone to secondary school together. I explained what I was doing. So we went through the place going from room to room, including toilets, praying the blood of Jesus and the blessing of God over each room.

Soon the girls and team arrived on the bus. The girls argued, fought, complained and were, on the whole, very different from any other group I had experienced before. The leaders found it hard going too. The girls were not interested in the Bible talks. Singing was difficult as they were very distracted. It was a hard slog. One night I even abandoned the meeting.

There were forty eight girls. We had two who needed a doctor as they were sick. Parents were informed and asked to come and collect them. We were told they had plans and literally 'a bed is a bed' so just keep them!

I was woken about 2 a.m. one morning and told by the Holy Spirit to go downstairs. I discovered two girls trying to run away. It was no problem to phone parents and ask them to come and collect them. These two girls were particularly disobedient and rebellious and had caused some trouble.

One of their fathers turned up in his big American car. All the girls gathered round and stared at the uniqueness of its size and breadth. The car had a problem because steam was pouring out from the bonnet. He got out and opened the bonnet and started to undo the cap. I bellowed loudly, 'Don't do that! Girls stand back!' but it was too late as hot water spurted out burning quite a few of the girls.

The burned girls were taken by the first aider to be treated while the other girls waved cheerio to the departing girls.

On the Sunday morning just before church, I checked the house was locked. The girls and leaders had started off walking to the local church. All of a sudden I discovered, because I had changed into my skirt, I had left the house keys in my jeans. Walking around the outside of the house, I spotted an open window beside the fire escape stairs. So climbing up the stairs, I climbed in through the window expecting to find myself in one of the dormitories. However, I was in a very dark room, the walls of which were covered in black wooden masks. Where was I?

I started to shout the names of the two women who ran the premises. No one answered.

Suddenly I heard one of them say, 'There is a burglar in the room. Get the poker!'

I shouted louder as I tried to tell them it was only me!

The door was opened gingerly and I was met with a raised poker!

When they saw it was me and they heard what I had done, they were relieved.

After church, we carried on with the programme for the afternoon's activities except I could not do what was planned for me to do as I was really sick and had to lie down. The rest of the leaders covered for me.

That night the leaders went to bed very early, the cook went to the evening service at the local church and I prayed in the kitchen.

What is going on Lord?

Will you show me what is happening?

I looked at all the cards my friends had sent to me at camp. The verses they contained were not the normal nice encouraging verses. One said, "For the weapons of our warfare are not carnal but mighty in God for pulling down strongholds." 2 Corinthians 10:4. Another card said God would fight for me.

I went into the hallway and noticed a big round brass plate with engraving on it above the meeting hall door. It looked strange. I had never noticed it until now. It had a mosque engraved on it which lay on its side and the people around it were upside down. God was telling me to pray over this plate. I did so. I heard

Him say to have the last meeting tomorrow night in the dining room.

When Susan the cook came back I asked her to join me in prayer. As we prayed, she said that I had not done what the Lord had asked me to. As she said this I had a picture of the garden gate at the end of the first floor corridor. The old ladies had sectioned off their living quarters by erecting a wooden garden gate that led to their four doors at the end of the corridor. I had climbed into one of their rooms earlier on and had to unbolt the gate to get out.

We knew we had to pray in that area. As we stood up, suddenly all the lights went out and it was incredibly dark. Taking my Bible, we walked along the lengthy dark hallway to the light switches at the front door and turned them on.

Then we walked up the stairs to the first floor and stood at the gate. Girls were out in the corridor upset and crying not knowing why. One of the young leaders asked what was wrong. The leaders encouraged everyone back into bed.

Praying in tongues and holding my Bible over the gate, not really knowing what else to do, the cook said "You have to go in". As I unbolted the gate I heard myself pray the blood of Jesus in this area. At that moment the cook fell to the floor holding her throat, gasping for air. What was wrong with her? She croaked that something was attempting to strangle her! Her lips started to turn blue.

I was enraged! How dare this thing touch her! I commanded it to leave her alone and all darkness and evil to go in Jesus name. She was fine and composed herself slowly. We stood amazed to see the wall of darkness before us lift up from the bottom of the floor and go towards the ceiling. As the darkness lifted, light came from the floor up. It was incredible! The door on the right which was always locked was now open. Shining the torch around the dark room we gasped as we saw long spears and dark wooden masks and skulls of dead animals. There were also stuffed figures. It was scary. It looked as if it was a trophy room! The volume of our praying went up a notch to say the least! As the torchlight filled the room, we heard bangs and bumps and crying from the dormitory above us. We ran upstairs.

The girls were crying, saying, "I'm scared", "I am frightened!", "I want my mum."

I declared quickly and loudly, 'Peace. Be still in Jesus' name!' The leaders who had joined us settled the girls, and we went to the dormitory next door as the girls there were disturbed and frightened. Again, after prayer, peace was restored and everyone was settled calmly.

The leaders wanted to know what was going on.

When I finally got to my room, the leader I was sharing with asked me why I had harshly banged the bedroom door open against the wall earlier on and then rattled chains beside my bed. I assured this lovely Brethren leader it was certainly not me! We prayed the blood of Jesus over the room and I commanded every evil spirit to leave and go to the cross. I had just learned another lesson in the 'School of the Holy Spirit!'

The next morning the girls behaved like little angels. It was breakfast without the usual quarrels or disagreements. Wonderful!

It was the second to last day and a bus came for the girls to visit a local tourist attraction. As I was going to be speaking that night, and had not prepared my talk, I stayed behind. My assistant leader took my car as we always had a car accompany the bus just in case it was needed.

After the bus had left I started to pray in the kitchen. About five minutes later, I saw my car coming up the driveway towards me. What was wrong now? The leader came and showed me there was a problem with my car boot. It was broken and would not stay shut.

By this time I had had enough. I simply put my hand on the broken lock, commanded it to work till it was fixed in Jesus' name. It closed and off she went to enjoy the most blessed day of the week!

I settled down to prepare the talk and when I was nearly finished, I was startled when a man appeared in the kitchen! He apologised for taking me by surprise and explained he was the leader of the next group coming after we left. He had been coming here from Ireland for seven years bringing his church group for a week, then his community group, then a youth group and then a school group. He and the cooks always came early, bought the food in the local cash and carry and stored it in the basement.

While he and the cooks unloaded their supplies, I finished the talk and started to prepare some tea and coffee for them, ready for when they had finished. The Holy Spirit said I should tell them what had happened the previous night.

They came into the kitchen and were drinking their tea and coffee and I told them the story of what had happened. The look on their faces was a picture of incredulity. I suppose it was no wonder!

They muttered something and thanked me and left quickly.

That evening was the best night ever. The girls were free to praise and worship. They listened attentively to the Word and many responded to the call and gave their lives to Jesus. The spiritual atmosphere was cleansed and Jesus was Lord.

When it came time for me to hand back the keys to the two old ladies before returning home, an opportunity arose for sharing the Good News about Jesus. They informed me that they did not need Jesus as they had their own religion. They brought it back with them from New Zealand where they had lived for many years. In fact they told me they had their own church in the house. I left heavy hearted. Truth is agreement with reality. So many people are deceived in various ways. Many people do have their own religion, beliefs and thoughts. Eternal destinies in heaven depend on them knowing the truth as it is stated in the Bible.

When I got home I took my car to the garage to have the boot lock fixed. The mechanic took one look at it, shook his head and said there was no way on earth this could have opened and closed as it was completely broken. I said "I know that but God is a God of miracles." Prayer makes the impossible possible.

About three months later I was preparing to go to Montrose to speak at an evening event. I knew that I had packed my bag earlier in the day with everything I would need. However, when checking it just before I set off, I discovered I had forgotten something and so rushed into my office above the S.U. Bookshop in Perth to collect it.

I parked my car on the double yellow line and ran into the shop, knocking a man down on my way in. I apologised profusely. When he stood up, it was the Irish chap I had met at camp. He said, "I was praying I would bump into you but not quite literally!"

He was on his way to the theatre at Pitlochry and wanted to tell me about his camp experience.

He said that in all the seven years he had brought groups to the house, this was the only year he had no fights, quarrels, disruptions, accidents, rebellion or illnesses. In fact this was the easiest and most enjoyable camp ever. All the leaders had agreed that there was a difference in the children and in the place. He shared the story with them. He had come to thank me for sharing what God had done to cleanse the place spiritually.

Truly our homes, workplaces and holiday places need spiritual cleansing by the blood of Jesus. After the lessons learned at this camp, I always pray the blood of Jesus over every place I stay.

I was asked to share what God was doing in Tayside at a meeting in Crieff. I was strongly encouraged by my boss, not to be late! I was busy that week and I fully intended to get around to organising a report to present at the meeting. Unfortunately I did not manage it.

Friday came before I knew it and I had two people drop in before and after tea. I prayed like mad all the way to Crieff, a half hour's journey away and I was already half an hour late when I set out! My praying in tongues would have raised the dead! The meeting would be well on its way by the time I arrived, late of course.

Walking into the room where the meeting was to be held, I was surprised to find no one there! I was confused till my boss came and said, "In all the years we have held this annual meeting, not once has it ever been suggested we start with tea first, until tonight. We were all seated when the director of Scripture Union stood up and announced, much to everyone's great surprise, "Let's start with tea and coffee first." So everyone was downstairs having tea and coffee!

I was so glad God had covered for me. I was humbled and wonderfully blessed. God can change longheld routines and habits in answer to our cries.

There was of course one problem left. I didn't have anything prepared to report. I remembered watching all the other staff workers with their facts and figures, photos and slides and graphs and pie charts, rhyming off so eloquently what they had been doing during the past months. I had zilch!

I explained my predicament to another staff worker, Kenny McKie, who suggested an interview. He would ask me questions; all I had to do was answer. It sounded perfect. Easy in fact!

He asked me what I thought about Scripture Union. I was honest and told him initially I thought it was dull and boring! People laughed! One thing I had learned was God is never dull or boring. He is full of adventures, out-of-the-boat, walking-on-water adventures! I had the opportunity to share some stories.

My eyes were opened to more of God's ways. Romans 11:33 says God's riches, wisdom, and knowledge are so deep that it is impossible to explain His decisions or to understand His ways. My God was no longer far off. He was interested in every aspect of my life, because He is always up close and personal.

Another time I was running late to go to a meeting in Edinburgh. I drove out of Perth, and saw, out of the corner of my eye, coloured things flying around my car on the left hand side of the pavement, then onto the grass verge. So I stopped and got out to discover my entire Filofax's contents had been blown about by the wind! How did they get outside the car? Suddenly I remembered. I had placed my Filofax on the car roof while I struggled with the key; my arms full of the things I needed to take with me. I had forgotten it was there and had simply driven off! What a mess, as notes, talks, songs, addresses and phone numbers were scattered everywhere. I scrambled along the verge and pavement quickly grabbing the coloured paper and stuffing them into a plastic bag. What a mess!

It reminded me of the words we speak. So easily can we mouth off and let loose our tongues and let words fly in every direction. Words which can wound, hurt, maim and destroy as well as words that can bless, encourage and build up. Once they are out, it is impossible to take them back! It was an important visual aid! By the time I got to Edinburgh I knew I was really late. Once again God worked a time miracle and the woman apologised for the meeting being late as there was a problem with the hall not being opened on time! Truly we have an amazing Father in heaven!

For three short years I travelled all over Tayside and beyond. I met so many fantastic people and saw so much of the beautiful countryside. I had a fabulous time. I got to see and hear what God was doing in answer to prayer. I saw lives touched through so many ordinary people. Mothers, dentists, teenagers, teachers, pupils and climbers all had testimonies of God touching their lives. Talk about a privilege!

I remember though there were many difficult and painful times too.

Angus area had a children's weekend. It did not go to expectation. At the 'post-mortem' problem areas were highlighted and discussed. It was crushing to hear my mistakes. It was however another learning curve. Changes would be required before I was allowed to organise another event.

I travelled home late that night, licking my wounds having a super wee pity party. My heart was heavy. It was my entire fault. I was to blame for the bad weekend. I was silent, sad and dejected. Just outside Dundee I heard, "Praise Me."

"O Lord," I sighed "I'm so sad I don't feel like praising You."

So I stayed silent as I travelled through all the roundabouts in Dundee to the other side.

I heard, "I haven't changed. I am worthy of praise. Praise is a choice not a feeling."

Through gritted teeth and with a sad, heavy heart and wet eyes I started to praise God. I sang slowly. I sang hesitantly with sobs puncturing the chorus till literally I broke through and realised my God is truly worthy of praise, adoration, exultation and love all the time, despite how I felt. Praise soared, singing out of the depths of my heart, my mouth full of love for God, and thankfulness pouring out of me for all His goodness. My desire was to please and glorify Him.

I was home in an instant, full of energy, joy and life! It was well after 11p.m. What was past was past, learn the lesson and move on!

Praise had exchanged my sadness for joy; as Isaiah 61:3 says "the garment of praise for the spirit of heaviness." What an exchange! I learned praise always chases the blues away. Yes, praise is also a choice. What a difference it makes; joy for sadness, lightness for heaviness, highs instead of lows!

As I was unpacking my bag, I heard the Holy Spirit say, "Go and visit Bill at Upper Springland."

Bill was a diver paralysed from the waist down in an accident. He went to our church. He lived in a special unit just outside Perth. It was like a village of individual flats under one roof with nursing staff on hand to help with people's physical needs.

It was 11.30 p.m. I was single. It didn't make Christian sense to visit a single guy at this time of night; by the time I got there it would be nearly midnight! I would probably not be allowed access.

"Go and visit Bill," persisted the Holy Spirit. Obedience is the key. It brings such pleasure to God. So I went, praying God would take care of all the thoughts in my head.

I was allowed entry. Bill was amazed and delighted to see me. He was in a state of deep depression and contemplating suicide. He had prayed that night if God wanted him to live to please send someone to visit him.

We laughed, cried and prayed. We gave thanks and enjoyed the presence of God. We both knew God had answered his prayer. A thought struck me on the way home. Would I have heard God say go and see Bill if I had stayed in a place of depression and self-pity? I actually believe that the night would have turned out very differently if I had! Truly God hears and His ways are unique and amazing.

Have you ever been ashamed to keep on going to God repenting of the same event, attitude or sin over and over again? I felt like I had committed the unforgivable sin and that God would not look at me.

Wrong thoughts can keep us from truth. If you know the truth you will be free indeed.

This night, as I repented once again for the same sin that happened years ago praying, "Please God will You forgive me for... O Lord you know ... "

"No, I don't know what you are on about! As far as the east is from the west, so far have I removed your sin." Psalm 103:12 and Micah 7:19 which says, "He will again have compassion on us, and will subdue our iniquities. You will cast all our sins into the depths of the sea."

"Who do you think you are to not forgive yourself when I, the God of all creation, forgave you the first time you repented?" I remembered that God sees us through the blood of Christ. All my sins past, present and future are covered by His precious blood.

Wow!

I was corrected and taught at the same time. If God forgave me, who am I to not forgive myself? Why do we allow the enemy of our faith to rob us and steal truth from us and cause us to fall into a pit of depression and agony of soul and for no good reason? Repent and move on quickly, just like King David did.

I learned that God really, truly loves me and as such He wanted me to know that if I confessed my sin, He is faithful and just to forgive me my sin and cleanse me from all unrighteousness (1John 1:9.) It took me ages to take God at His word. He means what He says.

How many times though have I missed Him because of rebellion, disobedience, selfishness and reason? Only God knows the thousands of times.

One night I went to a prayer meeting in Newport on Tay. It finished late and I was invited to stay in the profit room! It did not make sense to me. It did not cost me to stay with the lady so where was the profit in a room?

That night I had a dream. At breakfast, that was the first question I was asked. Did I have a dream? Yes, as a matter of fact I was driving a brown minibus and stopping at bus stops. I recognised a wooden bus stop made of logs and another bus stop beside the cinema in Perth. I saw lots of teenagers getting onto the bus.

It was not a 'profit' room but a 'prophet' room! When the bedroom was built a man of God, a prophet, stayed there and he anointed the room and prayed God would speak through dreams to everyone who stayed there. God speaks before He moves. The dream was so clear.

Next day, in the office I had phone call after phone call cancelling the SU pupils who had been booked in to an SU weekend we were having in the Nazarene church in Perth.

By the end of the day all the pupils had cancelled. The strange thing was I really believed that the weekend had to go ahead. The problem was that no pupils would be there, yet I had God's promise that He was going to do a new thing. Be ready!

Ian White had been booked to sing and Merv Milne, a local pastor, had agreed to speak. So after some serious prayer I decided, if God wanted this weekend to go ahead, He had to bring the teenagers.

On the Friday, my friend Ann, who had taught beside me in Clarkston, came up for the weekend. She was hoping for a restful weekend. At my flat! Are you serious?

The phone went and when I answered it, a pastor was offering me a minibus to use for the weekend. I asked, "What colour is it?"

"Brown," was the reply!

Faith is a funny thing. I had no teenagers booked in, but I had God's word and He said ; "Go ahead and have the weekend."

So, after tea on Friday, my friend came with me in the minibus. I knew where the wooden bus stop was. So I drove there. It was a village just outside Perth. There was usually a crowd of teenagers hanging around and so I asked them if they wanted to come to some meetings over a weekend in the Nazarene Church in Perth.

"Why not? It maybe won't be as boring as hanging around here."

So, in they piled. No mobile phones to call home to inform parents first! How times have changed for the better.

They were dropped off at the church with the leaders and then I went to the bus stop at the cinema and picked up some more teenagers. I went out three times with the bus. By the start of the night we had over thirty teenagers.

They talked while Ian White sang. They sat facing the walls; they sat behind the pillars in the room. The pastor got up to speak and to the natural eye it would have appeared no one was listening. But the conversations afterwards were proof that they had listened. They wanted to come back on the Saturday but they had different events on, which they were already committed to doing.

We were back to having no one for the Saturday meeting. My friend and I had a great time during the day. So, after agreeing in prayer, it was back to driving round Perth. It was a different group who came on the Saturday evening and they too enjoyed it.

Today if you drove round picking up teenagers and putting them in a minibus, you probably would be charged by the police.

I learned a lot about faith over that weekend. Faith is saying 'yes' when the circumstances say 'no'. Faith is believing all things are possible even when it looks impossible! Faith is looking beyond what is and trusting God for what will be. As Hebrews 11:1 says "Faith is the substance of things hoped for, the evidence of things not seen."

We had established a connection with the youths from the village bus stop and so I would go back and visit them. We would just stand talking. They liked to challenge. The oldest guy had a motorbike and the challenge was to give me a ride on the back of his bike. But not to worry, as he gave me a helmet borrowed from his mate. Praying in tongues, holding on as tightly as I could, we sped, at probably an illegal speed, along the country roads to Dundee and back! What fun! Not! It broke the ice and after that they 'accepted' me.

To look at me then, I wasn't the usual 'youth worker' type. I was old fashioned, frumpy and heavy. I never wore trousers, always a skirt. It never used to bother me, because when God hooked me up with people or teenagers, I always prayed I would decrease, get out His road so Jesus could be seen and heard. I did not want people to look at me so much as I wanted them to see Jesus in me. As usual, they ribbed me, made fun of me and carried on with their banter. But as well as this they would listen, and ask all kinds of questions about life with God and Jesus, and life without Him.

I visited the youth regularly and we felt we should hire a local village hall to have a weekly meeting. We tried all kinds of things; games, parachute activities, praise, and speakers, to name a few.

There was one young guy who always pushed the boundaries. While the majority would listen, he would do his utmost to disturb, mock, distract or destroy the night.

At the end of a very trying evening, and quite annoyed with "you know who", he smirked and gave me his usual lip as we left. I found myself turning round and saying very strongly, "You must be careful what you say. One day you too will die and Jesus is the only way to God." He took delight in answering me with a string of expletives. Did I not know he was young? He had years left before he died.

My father visited me one night a few weeks later. There was a knock at my flat door. I was shocked to find the two oldest guys from the bus stop group. I didn't know how they knew where I stayed and I must admit, I felt a bit surprised and uncomfortable.

"Hi guys. How are you?"

The oldest one said, "You haven't heard then?"

"No, I don't know what you mean?"

"Can we come in please? We have bad news."

My father's face was a picture, as these leather jerkined guys followed me into my living room. They sat down and told me that "you know who" had been at work, was sick, collapsed and choked on his vomit and died. He was still a teenager. He thought, as we all do, we have years left, plenty of time before we have to decide about Jesus. Some may have many years, but others may not!

Everyone went to the funeral in the local church which was filled to capacity. After the service his friends gathered round. They expected hope, answers and comfort. Unfortunately the minister was not a converted man and they could tell that from his sermon. They were deeply disappointed. They did not turn up after that. Seeds, however, were sown, and God knows everything.

Bad attitudes can kill the life we crave in the Spirit. I needed a car, to work in Inverness due to mine needing to be repaired. I was miffed to say the least that I had to collect the hire car on my day off. There was always something that had to be done on my days off. Today I really resented work intruding on my free time!

As I walked to collect the hire car from the garage, I let off steam walking and complaining at the same time. I did not want another day off doing 'work stuff.' However, I also knew that God was not glorified by my stinking attitude. Finally I repented and began to enjoy the walk cutting through the park on my way to doing 'work stuff.'

On arriving at the garage I was shocked to see a row of damaged cars against a wall. I saw the office door with broken glass. No one was there, so I shouted to attract attention. A man's voice called out telling me to please go in and wait as he would be there in two minutes.

My face fell as I entered the office. Papers were strewn everywhere, the seat was ripped and the desk was covered rather untidily with a mess of stuff.

My head said, "Cancel the hire car and find another one somewhere else!" Suddenly the garage owner came in and apologised for the state of the place. He had been burgled the night before and had his cars vandalised. He continued to say that I was not to worry as the car I was hiring was kept safe in the garage. It was ready for me.

The paperwork needed to be completed so he chatted as I wrote.

What did I do? I was an evangelist. What does that entail?

So I chatted informing him of what I did. He was interested in God and Jesus. He had heard of miracles and people being healed and he said he would love to see God work.

When I returned to the garage with the car on the Monday, I invited him to the church evening service the following week. He came and found it very interesting and came the following Sunday morning too.

Reinhard Bonnke was advertised as coming to Aberdeen on a Wednesday night in a few weeks' time. I told the garage owner about Christ for the Nations ministry. If he wanted to see miracles the opportunity was practically on his doorstep. However, I found there were quite a few other people, all unsaved, who wanted to go too. A minibus was filled and off to Aberdeen we went but it meant missing my regular Wednesday night Bible study. Being obedient to God can disrupt the regular routine and make you unpopular with man.

I figured I would drop everyone off at the cinema door in Aberdeen, go park the minibus and then find everyone inside. To my surprise on my return, I found the garage owner sitting down at the front beside a lady in a wheelchair. When he got off the minibus, a man asked if he could do him a favour and wheel the person in the wheelchair down to the front. No problem. He was then asked if he would like to sit beside them.

After praise and worship Reinhard Bonnke spoke from the Word of God. He gave a call for salvation and many went forward, including the garage owner. Everyone, who responded to the prayer of salvation, was taken to a room off to the side of the cinema.

When the new Christians came back, Reinhard Bonnke was praying for healing. He walked down to the people in the wheelchairs at the front. He stopped in front of a woman who had her hair set in a high bun.

She couldn't walk and had been housebound in bed for fifteen years.

"Stand in the name of Jesus!" he bellowed in his pleasant German accent.

She put her hands on the chair and stood up rather slowly and very shakily. She stepped forward.

"Legs be strengthened!" shouted Reinhard and she stopped wobbling.

He told her to make her way up the stairs to the stage as God was not finished with her. This she did.

Reinhard went among the people and many were healed in Jesus' name. He then went on the stage and prophesied over the newly healed lady that she would give her testimony around the world. He told her to run in Jesus' name. The woman on stage ran across it, more than once.

A friend saw her years later in Romania and another friend encountered her in America too. She also came to a local church to testify how God had healed her.

Many on the minibus that night were saved, including a close friend of the garage owner. Both came to the church and it was lovely to see them read their Bibles and pray.

One day I decided to paint my dirty kitchen ceiling and discovered it was too much. I sat down and prayed, my arms and neck badly aching, "O Lord, help me please." Literally five minutes later the doorbell rang and there stood the garage man and his pal. My ceiling was finished in no time. God is so good!

Unfortunately, sad news followed not too much later. The garage owner's friend died in a tragic way. His mother was comforted that at least she knew he was in a far better place.

Divine appointments come in many shapes and sizes and it's vital our hearts remain open. Be ready for anything was always running through my head.

I was in Inverness one particular Saturday. There had been street work during the day. I had parked my car in an NCP car park not too far away. However, the chap organising the outreach asked me to come back to the church and he offered me a lift. I thought nothing about it at the time and so got a lift to the church. After tea we were in the church hall preparing for the youth outreach. The meeting was minutes away from starting when into my head came the thought, "I need to go and get my car. Now!"

So I told the organiser where I was going. He thought I had lost the plot. I was needed to talk to the youth. Nevertheless, I had to get my car.

When I left the hall, I realised I did not have a clue where I was or where my car was for that matter.

Praying quickly and asking the Holy Spirit to guide me, I turned left, right, left at His prompting. I walked down this street not recognising anything when suddenly a woman came up alongside me. She looked ill and was gasping badly for breath. She slumped against the wall clutching her chest, desperate for breath. I quickly said that I was a Christian and could I pray for her. She nodded yes and I prayed. "God heal this lady and put air in her lungs now!"

She took a deep breath, followed by another. She straightened up and stood on her feet, no longer leaning against the wall.

"What did you do to me?" she asked. I told her I was a Christian and I believed in the power of God to heal. She went on to tell me that her husband had recently left her and the children. She had taken them to the cinema but then felt she was having an asthmatic attack. To her horror she discovered her inhaler was in her car, so she left the children in someone's care and tried to get to her car. Only she knew she could not make it. We spoke about Jesus' love for her even though her husband had rejected her; God's love for her would always remain. I gave her a gospel tract I had in my pocket and she took it saying she would read it later. She wanted to get to her car and back to her children. I told her I was trying to get to the NCP car park. She pointed to a huge sign sticking out of the wall near us. I had not seen it at all. She said her car was also there, so we walked in together. Guess whose car was right beside hers? Talk about the timing of God. He surely knows how to set us up for adventures in the ordinary things of life.

How often have we been guilty of trying to help God and do things in our own strength? I was really good at getting in God's way! He doesn't like sweat as it involves striving and not resting. He was working on me, encouraging me to stop trying so hard in my own strength and instead yield all to Him, allowing Him to do it through me. Did Jesus Himself not say that, "I do nothing on My own?"

An invitation to speak at a youth meeting came in. No matter how hard I prayed I could not get any leading on what to prepare. The meeting was fast approaching and still no clue came as to what I should speak on. Now I was anxious, yet I also had an incredible peace at the same time. This had never happened before, and it was not a comfortable feeling. How often do we like feeling good, comfortable and in control? I kept praying in the Spirit.

Barry, the leader of the group, invited me to tea before the meeting and over the meal casually informed me that it was now an open meeting. So as well as the teenagers, parents and friends would also be there! And still I had nothing. Not a single thought came to me.

The hall was packed. Every seat was filled with a mixture of teenagers and adults. I prayed hard in tongues, "Help, O Lord! Help!"

After praise and worship I stood up, looking at all their faces looking back at me expectantly. Nothing was in my head or heart for that matter. Silence! Ages seemed to pass, then all of all sudden I heard the Holy Spirit say, "Get out of the way. I want to speak." In my simple understanding, instead of standing in the middle at the front, I took one large step sidewards.

By faith I opened my mouth and let the Holy Spirit speak through me. I was gob-smacked as I knew it was most definitely Him and certainly not me! Giving the altar call at the end, nearly everyone stood up. I thought they had misunderstood so I asked them to sit down. Again, I asked if they were sure they wanted to repent and give their lives to Jesus and make Him Lord, to come out to the front.

All except the three Christians running the meeting came out! It was a stupid suggestion really, because there was no space at the front and to say it was rather cramped was an understatement!

A lot were Roman Catholic adults. I met some of them months later and I was greatly encouraged to hear how they were really connecting with Jesus and hungry for His word. Some had moved church in obedience to God's leading. It is wonderful what God can do when we get out of the way!

Many times since then He has taken over and I get out of His way, trusting Him because I now know very well Jesus did it all the time. John 14:10 "The words that I speak to you I do not speak on My own authority; but the Father who dwells in Me does the works."

Yes, following Jesus is all about letting Him lead.

Moving On
From Scripture Union
to PWAMM

I loved working for Scripture Union in Tayside. However, towards the end of my third year I kept reading and hearing about having a new job, moving on, leaving work, living by faith and trusting God. So I knew and recognised something was changing. Only God's plans and timetable are what we should be concerned about. Sometimes though it's not convenient when we want to stay and He says move on. It's quite amazing how He leads.

For about two years, I went to the church that People with a Mission Ministries (PWAMM) had, which was based in the Christian Centre in Perth. I was invited to join PWAMM's pastors in America for two weeks in the November of my third year in SU. The idea was that I would help to look after their two young daughters while they were at speaking engagements.

In one place we stayed in a retired pastor's house while he was away seeing his family. The book beside my bed was entitled 'The Favour of God'. The book was about how the Lord wants to give us success because it makes Him attractive to others when we acknowledge Him as the source. But in order to see the favour of God fully we have to pursue God continuously; approach Him with the right motives and always keep a right attitude. If we do, we can experience supernatural increase and promotion, restoration of everything the enemy has stolen, honour in the midst of our enemies, great victories in spite of great odds, recognition, even when we seem the least likely to be selected and preferential treatment and an avoidance of some battles, as God will fight them for us.

It was a brilliant book and I absorbed the truth it highlighted to me. I had never even heard of the favour of God. However, I was willing to test this new truth.

During my time in America, I was invited to accompany a woman from Prison Fellowship to visit a prison. My pastor would visit the male prison while I went to the female prison next door. The actual prison I went into was a rectangular bricked room with one door. Inside there were no brick walls, only bars. Each cell was supposed to have two beds and a toilet but they were cramming three and sometimes four women into the small cells. The prisoners were not allowed to wear bras in case they used them to strangle themselves, inmates or officers. We were shown to the area used as a refectory. It had a bench with attached seats which we sat on. The officer announced that anyone who wanted could attend the service. A few women came, introductions were made and testimonies shared.

One I really remember was that of an older Christian woman who had murdered the wealthy old man she cared for. She poisoned him over a period of time, changing his will and leaving her as sole benefactor. After his death, the old man's family were suspicious and got his body exhumed. The poison was discovered, she was found guilty and sentenced. To listen to her speak, she showed no remorse and was angry with the family for stopping her becoming wealthy! The amazing thing was that she claimed that she was a born again believer! She was so motivated to get wealthy that it influenced her thoughts leading her to commit murder and suffering the consequences that followed. How we need to have the mind of Christ influencing our every thought and decision!

Once again I was out of my depth. Another prisoner felt really bad about her crime and was remorseful but her problem was she could not accept the fact that God could forgive her. The Prison Fellowship woman then told a modern parable to help her understand that God's love and His forgiveness are amazing and they cover every sin committed.

She spoke of a beach where a small boy dug a wee hole in the sand with his plastic spade as he filled his bucket. Then moving on, she described a man with a spade digging a big hole in the sand with a mound of sand at his side. Then she said at the end of the beach there was a JCB using a bucket to dig down deep, making a massive hole in the sand.

The prisoner said her crime felt like it had been committed by the JCB because it caused a lot of damage. Next we were all told to keep that picture in our minds, and watch the tide come in. What happened to the bucket sized hole, the spade sized hole and the JCB sized hole? The tide had filled them all in! There were no holes left at all on the smooth beach. She went on to share about how powerful the blood of Jesus is in cleansing us from all sin. Just like the tide, the blood of Jesus washes all our sins completely away. I enjoyed this parable and so did the women but no one responded to the offer of having their sins forgiven. Maybe another time they did. God knows.

When I boarded the flight home from America, I was quietly sitting in my seat minding my own business when a very large businessman in a very expensive suit loomed over me and told me in no uncertain terms that I was in his seat and could I move! No please about it! I got out my ticket and found I was sitting in the correct seat and that I was quite happy here thank you very much. Well you should have heard the commotion he caused! He wanted that seat! He always sat in that seat and he wanted it now! Spoilt little boy!

The stewardess came and whispered to me quietly that she would find another seat but would I please move to keep this customer quiet? She showed me to another seat.

I began to chat with the woman beside me who was on her way to Edinburgh to see her old father. She was about forty and had been diagnosed with cancer. There was no cure and she had been given months to live. She was a Catholic lady with a husband she had married about seven years previously and they had two young sons under six. She was on her way home to tell her father the news in person and to say goodbye. She was terrified of dying. What had just happened? The businessman had his seat and I had God's seat. He had set me up again!

Naturally we spoke about Jesus and what He had done on Calvary for us. She was introduced to Jesus. She was not only saved but baptised in the Spirit too. We then prayed for healing. Many times I often wonder what happened to her. One day in heaven I shall look forward to a lot of catching up.

By the beginning of my fourth year in Perth, I had left SU and was working with PWAMM, living by faith. It was a huge learning curve. For the first six months I had no regular wage or financial arrangement. It was God only! I saw Jehovah Jireh, God my provider, supply my needs. I prayed and sought the Lord for all my needs. He gave me a promise to stand on. "I will always meet your needs but not necessarily all your wants." I learned quickly the difference between needs and wants! It is surprising how we can mix them up and it takes God, demonstrating the truth about each one, to differentiate between a need and a want. We need food and shelter but we do not need new jewellery!

I had been going to the church for two years by the time I became a PWAMMER. The church was a Full Gospel Church or Pentecostal Church. When I first went there the praise and worship was quite different from other churches I had visited. For a start they lifted their hands when they sang. It was strange. No matter how hard I tried I felt odd at the thought of lifting my hands up into the air above my head when I sang. So I did not!

I had been going there for a number of weeks and the pastor suggested I try raising my hands at home when I praised God. I could do that in the privacy of my flat.

I read the verses in the Bible and found it is an age-old practice.

Psalm 63:4 "I will bless You while I live; I will lift up my hands in Your name."

Psalm 134:2 "Lift up your hands in the sanctuary, and bless the Lord."

Then the pastor shared that football supporters threw their hands in the air when their team scored a goal, but Jesus had done something far more incredible. He died in my place and opened the way for me to go to heaven. Now that was a far superior thing than a silly leather ball filled with air being kicked between two wooden posts!

In the cold light of the revelation of just what Jesus had done two thousand years ago, I was free to praise my Lord with both hands raised far above my head. I fully appreciated what He had done for me.

There was a special speaker from England one night. I went to listen to this woman, who had a van with a Christian library in the back. She travelled around rural villages. The first week she came into a village, she would open the back of her van and offer local passers-by a Christian book to read. The following week she went back, spoke to each person about the book they had read and whenever possible, answered any questions they had. Then they changed their books. Eventually she was offered a cup of tea in a home and from there house groups were set up in many villages. What a simple idea I thought!

As she spoke I had a picture of me on wheels going round an outline of Scotland. At the time I failed to see the significance of this, my first vision from God. It was prophetic but lost on me at that point.

Johnny Hamilton, an ex-pastor from Gorebridge and then an itinerant speaker, came to speak. The night before the meeting I had a dream, another God dream! I dreamed I was pregnant and I could feel my huge stomach. I knew but I knew that there was no husband and I had to tell my father and pastor. Talk about a Mary moment!

"How can this be?"

I woke up the next morning still pregnant in my mind and when I brushed my teeth suddenly realised I was not! Talk about relief! That night Johnny spoke at the meeting and as always gave an anointed Word.

I was introduced to Johnny after the meeting and he was told I was a new PWAMMER. He took my hand and simply said "Congratulations my dear! You are pregnant!" My pastor's wife's face was a picture! I must admit so was mine! He explained I was pregnant with a God-given ministry and told me that at the set appointed time God would birth it.

All this talk was strange to me: religion versus the Spirit once again. It was incredible knowing God knew everything. When my rent was due money would come in and petrol, food, road tax and insurance, all were taken care of. Everything was paid on time to the penny. My first miracle of provision was my need of a car. The S.U. car was returned at the end of my time with S.U. in the December.

One night I got a phone call after tea. Are you in tonight? I am bringing a car to you. I was given one, surplus to their requirements, but completely suitable for my needs. That car was great. It covered thousands of miles and then it broke down. The garage at the end of the road quoted £200 to fix it. Money failed to come in. I borrowed a friend's car or walked.

Weeks went by but still no money came in. I prayed on. I went in my friend's car to visit my father, who lived an hour away. When I approached his driveway I thought he had a visitor as there was a black Volkswagen sitting at the back door. "Who's in?" I enquired.

"Nobody."

"Whose car is that?"

"Yours!" he smiled.

He went on to say that his neighbour had taken his car, a black Volkswagen Jetta, for an MOT and it failed due to an oil filter not being up to scratch. He went out and bought a new car, came back and asked my dad to get rid of his old car and to give it to me! £9 fixed the oil filter which was fitted by my dad and I had a new car.

When I went to church the next Sunday, one of the guys came up and offered to buy my old car as he needed a running around car for his wife since their family had just increased with the arrival of a new baby!

He was told it needed repairing. Not a problem and he gave me money for my old car! I had a new car and money in my bank. I felt incredibly blessed. Truly the ways of God are past finding out about. Sometimes we need to give God space and time to do things His way.

I had a marvellous opportunity to go to the National Exhibition Centre in Birmingham to hear Reinhard Bonnke speak at a huge conference he was holding.

A group went from Perth by bus. We stayed in a hotel and had an eye-opening time among the thousands of people there. I had never attended such a large gathering ever. I went to an amazing prayer meeting before the evening event. Hundreds of Christians gathered and Suzette Hattingh led us in prayer for the meeting that night. At the end of the prayer meeting, she chose people to sit around the outside edge of the large auditorium. Their task was to pray in tongues while the meeting was in progress. I had never heard anything like it.

That evening the praise and worship was excellent as thousands of Christians praised God. Reinhard Bonnke came on the stage and spoke. At the ministry time he operated in 'words of knowledge'. They were specific and amazing, because God was revealing facts about people and their situations that only He could know.

He said there was a man from the back left hand side of the auditorium who did not want to come when his friend asked him earlier this evening. He told the man that as he sat listening, he was experiencing his heart racing. "Come now and receive Jesus," Reinhard invited. No one came. He waited. No one came. He said "Your name is Andrew." Andrew ran from the top seated area all the way down to the front. He ran to meet Jesus in front of everyone.

Another word of knowledge came. He said a lady on the right hand side, got bad news from her consultant that day. She has cancer. "God wants to heal you." No one came. He added, "You had a blue dress on before you came out tonight and at the last minute you changed it for a red dress." This woman in a red dress stood up and came down for prayer. Many people were healed. It was wonderful.

One evening in particular, was most amazing. At the end of his talk Reinhard called out pastors and prayed for them. Then he called out those who were called to be evangelists. I went forward for prayer along with hundreds of others. That night was like a commissioning prayer with each one being sent out to make disciples of all nations. When prayed for I was deeply moved.

PWAMM had a Christian bookshop, café, crèche and church. They had a vision to take the power and presence of God into the communities around Scotland. At the set appointed time a double decker bus was acquired and kitted out with the gospel message illustrated on boards downstairs with a seated area upstairs. It seemed to take ages before it was finally ready to go on the road. In actual fact the team needed to be prepared as well as the bus.

Bill Subritzky came to do a huge conference in England. I was blessed when God made it possible for me to attend that conference.

Healing and deliverance were being taught. People were prayed for and I was astounded at the physical difference that was instantly evident in people. I remember one very dark, heavily oppressed young man who, after receiving prayer for deliverance, changed and his face shone and became full of light. He testified later how he had been touched by Jesus and had been set free. That conference launched me into a season of further research into healing and deliverance.

Books would be given to me and I would study God's Word learning that with one word Jesus told the demons to go. The Bible is full of stories of Jesus dealing with demons. It is funny how cinemas can portray demons running rampant in films and nothing is said. Young people and children even enjoy them on TV and games consoles and nothing is said. People in African or Indian countries can experience the chaos demons can bring when they open their lives or homes to them. They readily accept the reality of them, yet the Western church panics and nearly faints at the thought of the existence of demons. God was preparing me for what He knew lay ahead.

A church in Dundee was having a speaker called Gwen Shaw one weekend. I took a car load there. She certainly moved under the power of the Holy Spirit.

When we were leaving, Myra, a lady I knew from Clydebank came up to me and simply said, "You will be used to set the captives free."

The bus was finally ready for the road and so were we. Missions were organised all over Scotland. Contact was made with churches or fellowships. Permission was sought from Police or councils to set up the bus in a street, a car park, a school or even a local park. Initially local shops would give us a power supply. Later on we would have our own generator.

'The Challenger Bus' as it was known, opened its doors throughout Scotland. Passers-by were invited aboard to be asked 'The Big Question'. "Do you know where you will spend eternity?" or to answer the Challenge "Who do you say Jesus is?" or "Do you have a need we can pray for?"

Many people came on board happily listening to the Good News, asking questions, receiving prayer, or even having a cup of tea, served from our very own little kitchen upstairs. There were many lives touched by the love of Jesus, the power of the Holy Spirit and the Word of God.

There was one woman who came on board in the morning when the bus was really quiet. She had much pain from many bad relationships. She tried many ways to alleviate her broken heart and still she was in agony till she met Jesus. She repented and Jesus touched her and she was set free. Literally her life changed because Jesus truly makes a difference.

The Challenger bus visited schools too. It was a busy time when children came on at lunchtime, cramming upstairs to listen to the gospel, then going off to get their lunch before the next group came on.

One lunchtime we counted nearly two hundred pupils had visited us. Busy indeed!

The team would also take school assemblies. At one school assembly we spoke on Zacchaeus. I asked for help and chose an upper primary pupil to play Zacchaeus in the drama. We did not know that the boy chosen had been caught stealing from the tuck shop that very morning! He was excellent as 'Zacchaeus'. The school, including Zacchaeus, got the message. The teachers thought we knew about his misdemeanours. We didn't, but God did. Zacchaeus changed!

On another mission the bus was outside Glasgow. In the evenings we would have loads of teenagers come on board full of questions, many with attitude and all of them with stories to tell: sad homes, loveless relationships, broken families, neglect, drugs, drink, sexual or physical abuse, poverty, hunger and loneliness. The stories broke our hearts to listen to them. Other teenagers and children had close families full of material possessions but no boundaries or discipline or love.

On many nights the teenagers were challenging! There was laughter, tears and plenty of chat or swearing! This particular evening was no different from any other. The gospel was spoken as it usually was.

However, the next morning one of the mothers came angrily up to me demanding 'a pound or two of flesh'! She was a Church of Scotland mum who wanted to know why her daughter was being lied to. The lie being that only those who are born again go to heaven and those who do not know Jesus as Lord and Saviour go to hell.

She took exception to the thought of hell and did not believe in it. As long as you went to church you were guaranteed entrance into heaven; That was the truth according to mum! What could I say to that? I prayed quickly and asked the Holy Spirit to speak through me.

"Do you read your Bible?"

"No." she said.

"Try reading these verses and come back and tell me what God's Truth says."

She did not come back, which was a pity.

So many people have their own ideas, notions, opinions, thoughts, beliefs, and often times the truth of God's Word is lacking and they perish as a result of their ignorance. If someone is offended maybe they need to be in order to make them seek truth for themselves.

We as a team enjoyed visiting all types of churches, fellowships and schools.

On one mission to Govan we had a mum and her dog come on board the bus. While speaking to her upstairs, she quickly got up and ran down the stairs. Back up she came dragging one of her daughters whom she had noticed passing by the bus. A little later, mum ran off the bus again and brought her son back up with her. All heard the gospel. The mother had mental health issues. The family had drink and drug problems.

That evening, the church hosting the bus, put on an evening outreach meeting. Sure enough, the mother brought all her children including some who had not been on the bus. All were born again. The father had previously left home and when he heard that they were having a party every week, he came back wanting to know where they were getting the money. He could not believe that the so called 'party' was actually a Bible study! Later on he too became a Christian. They later served in a soup kitchen having many opportunities to share their testimonies, for such was the radical transformation of the family.

At church in Perth people came from all over Scotland to the church meetings and conferences that were held regularly. There was once a man who sat in the café waiting patiently for his friends. I got chatting to him, all the while listening to both what he was saying and also what the Holy Spirit was whispering. He had recently heard about the baptism of the Holy Spirit. Because of the teaching at his church, that the gifts had died and no longer existed today, he had closed his mind to it all. But he still had questions and certainly peace eluded him. I had just read a modern parable which I shared with him.

Ulf Eckman, a speaker told a story of how he and his wife went to America. There was a huge Christian conference with thousands in attendance. The speaker shared the platform with another two men, big names in Christian circles.

One of the people there, a Christian publisher, was very deeply touched through their ministry. He invited the three speakers and their wives to go to his warehouse and take whatever Christian books they wanted. There was no limit to the number of books they could take.

The speaker and his wife took two suitcases the day they had all agreed to meet at the warehouse. Each of them went along the aisles of books. The speaker and his wife collected piles of books which they asked if they could leave on the counter till they were finished.

When the allotted time was over, all returned to the counter. As the speaker and his wife packed all their books into their two suitcases, they thought of friends, family and church members who would be blessed to receive these Christian books. They noticed what the other two speakers had taken.

One speaker held one book. The other speaker had three books.

He was amazed. He asked them why on earth they had only chosen one book and three books.

One of them said that he only wanted one. The other replied he felt greedy if he took more. The speaker summed it up really well.

"You were told you could have any amount you wanted. There was no limit!"

He went on to describe this story as a picture of Christians in churches.

There are many who are hungry and thirsty and want everything they can from God and His word. They in turn want to bless everyone they can. However there are some Christians who are happy with the little they have and wouldn't dream of appearing greedy. Still there are others who have tried a little more but don't press in to take hold of the much more God has for them and so many fail to receive blessing through them.

When I had finished telling the story to the man I asked which person he represented. He said the 'one book' speaker.

We looked at Acts chapters 1 to 3. Imagine the last words of Jesus to His disciples. Acts 1:8, "But you shall receive power when the Holy Spirit has come upon you; and you shall be witnesses to Me in Jerusalem, and in all Judea and Samaria, and to the end of the earth."

In Acts1:4-5 Jesus commanded them not to depart from Jerusalem but to wait for the promise of the Father which, He said, "you have heard from Me; for John truly baptised with water, but you shall be baptised with the Holy Spirit not many days from now."

Jesus knew His disciples, then and now, need a power beyond themselves for service and ministry in His Kingdom on earth. The Great Commission in Matthew 28:19-20 is to go into all the world and make disciples of all nations. This is a task we need His power to accomplish.

Being filled or baptised with the Holy Spirit is God's command in Ephesians 5:18 "Be filled with the Spirit."

When we had finished reading God's Word, it came down to a step of faith in obedience to God. The enemy of our faith hates us being filled with the Holy Spirit and uses fear to try and stop us. But if God is love and God is good why do we fear?

Some people find it so easy to ask and receive, but those with bitterness and unforgiveness or who have dabbled in occult practices or who are very religious can sometimes find it a bit harder to receive the baptism in the Spirit. Repenting of these things brings an enabling to simply receive by faith.

He prayed a simple prayer, "Heavenly Father, at this moment I come to You. I thank You that Jesus saved me. I pray that the Holy Spirit might come upon me. Lord Jesus I ask You to baptise me now in the Holy Spirit. I receive the baptism in the Holy Spirit right now by faith in Your Word. May I be empowered for service from this day forward. Thank You Jesus for baptising me in Your Holy Spirit. Amen!"

As the disciples received their new heavenly language, so he praised God and he too spoke in his spiritual prayer language. He was now free to communicate with God in his new language whenever or wherever he wished. It was the start of discovering the ways of God outside of a religious box.

A beautiful and precious experience which I will never forget happened one night on my way to Perth from my father's house. It was raining.

Rainbows have always blessed me because of the beautiful reminder of God's covenant promises. As I drove on the dual carriageway heading for Perth, there was a very strong rainbow up ahead of me. Then an amazing thing happened; there was a white car in front of me and as I drove the spectrum of colours shone on the white car. It was as if the end of the rainbow was on the road and the white paint showed the spectrum beautifully as I drove through it. It was awesome!

It was unbelievable to drive for miles watching the red, orange, yellow, green, blue indigo and violet show up on that car. I praised God for His promises. It was a unique experience driving as it were through a rainbow!

As soon as I arrived in Perth, I went to a Full Gospel Businessmen's meeting. The speaker, David Antrobus, was from England and there were a lot fewer people there than normal for some reason. He shared testimony and ministered at the end.

He gave a word of knowledge about a person who was in pride. I knew it was me! He said this pride was an abomination to God and he gave a call to repent and come out now for prayer. I sat paralysed, knowing God was revealing my pride not only to me but to everyone in the room.

He waited till someone responded. I sat motionless with my heart playing a big bass drum which surely must have been heard by everyone there.

Proverbs 8:13 says, "The fear of the Lord is to hate evil; pride and arrogance and the evil way and the perverse mouth I hate."

God was showing me He hated my pride. It was an awful thought.

Again the speaker waited and said he knew who it was and that he could pick the person out. He said pride was a sin and it was stopping God from doing what He wanted. Talk about a revelation on the spot! I knew but I knew, my pride was like a stench in the nostrils of God. I was broken. I repented and walked forward. Forgiven and cleansed by the Blood of the Lamb, I learned a valuable lesson. Keep humble before God. I must always decrease and He must increase. I should live daily, giving God all the praise and all the glory because truly I can do nothing apart from Him. Never touch the glory that belongs to God only.

It was a necessary lesson when I saw myself as God saw me. He reveals to us what we are really like in our heart of hearts. He sets up the circumstances to show us what He already knows is there in our hearts, but that we are ignorant of. The incredible thing is He always loves us perfectly in spite of necessary corrections. He is, after all, our Father.

There was a special speaker one time in Perth and I strongly felt led to invite my father. Unfortunately he was saying an emphatic 'no' to the invitation. However the sense that he was to come would not leave me. Weeks went by and still he was not biting! I prayed and asked God what I was to do. My father had fallen some nine months before and had been left with pain all over his body due to damage to his central nervous system. He was in agony. This speaker was used in evangelism and healing.

The Holy Spirit prompted me to tell my father's friend who was not saved either. His friend said to just book two tickets.

The evening came and I phoned my dad one last time at 6 p.m. He stated once more very emphatically he would not be there! But God!

My father's friend phoned him and told him he was taking him out for a meal. He was told to grab his jacket as he would be there in ten minutes to collect him. By the time I had arrived at the hotel, they were both already seated!

They both listened attentively. The speaker shared about trouble with his business, and bankruptcy among other things. This was them both to a T! At the ministry time my father said he was going home. I encouraged him to go for prayer or I would ask the speaker to come to him. No way! He was going home! I said I would stand in for him and ask for prayer as he walked to the car park. When he put his hand on the car door handle he froze. His friend asked him what was wrong. All the pain was gone! It did not come back. That night my father was completely healed and his friend saved. About a month later his friend was found dead in bed. He had had a massive heart attack. The timing of God is absolutely amazing and we must press in when we know what He is saying.

Another time not long after this Full Gospel Businessmen's meeting, my father came to hear Frank Smith who had been a miner like him. My dad was interested in hearing his story. Before the meal we sat at a table with two empty seats. There was a lady who sat opposite us. She told us how her daughter had told her about this meeting and had encouraged her to come along. The woman also told us she had had a mild angina attack down the street earlier that afternoon and was not feeling very well as a result. During the meal the woman, Sylvia, felt more unwell and wanted to go home. My father told me to get the car and take her home but the Holy Spirit was telling me, "Keep her here as she will be healed". Praying hard, I encouraged her to be at peace and wait till she could get prayer.

The testimony was great and my father could identify with the speaker's time down the mine.

At the ministry time the woman responded to the call for salvation. Then she went forward for healing and asked me to accompany her as she was feeling scared. As she had trouble standing, she sat on a chair and waited till the speaker came along the prayer line to her. When she was asked what was wrong with her, she told him she had heart trouble, arthritis, blood trouble and a few other ailments. Turning to me the speaker said, "You pray for her".

"I don't know how to!"

"Just pray and ask God to heal her".

Shaking in my shoes I did pray and ask God to heal her.

When I had finished I looked at the speaker expecting him to pray properly for her. He didn't!

"Aren't you going to pray properly for her?" I asked.

His reply startled me. "My dear girl, remember it's not us who does the healing. It is God. Come here with me and pray for this man".

I joined him in praying for other people waiting for prayer. When I came back to my seat later on, the woman was sitting down opposite my father. Her face was no longer pale and sickly but rosy red and healthy.

"Look!" she said, as she stood up and then sat down.

She repeated herself. I honestly did not know what I was looking at. I thought perhaps her underskirt was hanging down under her skirt but it wasn't. I finally gave in and said I didn't know what she wanted me to look at! She demonstrated sitting down and standing up quite a few more times.

"I am healed!" she said. All her pain was gone and she had no stiffness whatsoever!

I was absolutely gobsmacked. I knew God could heal, but for the first time I knew that He could use anyone, including me, to pray for someone and they could experience healing. Because the meeting had gone on for so long, she had missed her bus home, so I gave her a lift after I had said goodbye to my father.

When we arrived at her house her daughter was leaning out of the window as she was worried about her mother being out late as this was an unusual occurrence. The woman got out of the car, and then the daughter came and sat in my car! Very strange!

"But Mum, you get out of the car like this." And the daughter slowly demonstrated how slowly and awkwardly her mother usually got out of a car.

"What's happened to you?" she asked.

"God healed me tonight. Race you to the house." Mum won!

I met this same woman weeks later and she told me that God had healed her of all her ailments much to the doctor's astonishment. She shared her testimony with him.

I discovered years later that the speaker, Frank Smith, spoke to my father that night. He told him that someone had shared the gospel with him underground. "How did you know? I have never told a soul not even my wife!" It turned out that the older man my father worked with was a Christian who spoke to him many times about Jesus. My father always resisted.

God knows everything and we cannot hide a thing from Him. Life can sometimes be hectic as a Christian. Church activities keep us busy with little room or next to no time to connect with others outside our circle. How many times do we fail to lead a balanced life? It is easy when you love your job to fail to rest properly. That was a common problem I suffered with from time to time. Sometimes I would be 'all peopled out' and would withdraw from everyone.

One of these times, it was decided I would visit my sister in York, so I took the train. Sitting in the compartment, there was a young guy sitting opposite. He was quite chatty. I did not want to engage in any conversation whatsoever, to the point I was on the rude side.

He got up and left at his station.

The Holy Spirit said, "Suppose you were his last chance to hear the gospel."

I knew immediately I had blown it! I felt dreadful. I did not fully appreciate at the time that a God opportunity has, as it were, a sell-by date. Usually it's 'now' or it's gone!

Failure to see people through Jesus' eyes means our agenda wins and His will does not enter the scene.

Walking in the Spirit means choosing to yield moment by moment to the leading of the Holy Spirit, even if it is inconvenient or totally off our agenda or we are all 'peopled out'!

Needless to say, I said sorry to God and prayed for help to be obedient next time. It made me think how often do we fail to see, recognise or engage with ordinary folk in our path, leaving a Kingdom footprint on their lives or enabling another link in the Kingdom chain to be added.

I remember a challenge was issued to me that was huge. God has His ways of making what He is saying very clear and confirms it with no room for doubt. I kept reading different sources of Daniel's 21-day fast. I met two ladies who had recently done a Daniel fast. I just thought it was interesting, till I finally got the message. God wanted me to do a Daniel fast!

My mind could only see the impossibilities. I was a big girl who loved her food; that was very evident! To go for twenty one days with only fruit juice seemed inconceivable! But the choice is always - will I be obedient or not?

So I yielded and said I was willing, if He enabled me. If I fasted for one day then I would follow it with another twenty. That first day was odd to say the least. Nothing went according to my plans at all. I had early morning phone calls to attend to and left without breakfast. Lunch was late and before I could eat it, I was called away. I didn't get home till very late and was about to eat a plate of cornflakes when I just happened to glance at the kitchen clock. It was 4 minutes past midnight. I put the spoon down and the cornflakes went in the bin.

I was committed to a 21 day fast. I drank only fruit juice and prayed, sought and served God. The following days were filled with energetic activities and many moments of quiet times and work as normal and not once did I feel sick or lacking. God is so good. He enabled me to be obedient to His Word. It was the first of many.

The next time He said to undertake a Daniel fast was while I was on holiday with my friend Eileen in Fuengerola in Spain. Again I read about Daniel, and wondered if this was God's will for me now. We went to a wee English speaking church on the Sunday afternoon and the speaker that Sunday was from England. Guess what he spoke about?

It was time for the fast to start immediately, whether on holiday or not. God's timings can seem inconvenient but we must remember He calls the shots, not us. During the fast I kept getting words on war, battles, spiritual warfare and the enemy at work. Rather strange I thought as I would walk praying along a lovely beach, sit in the sun and read my Bible or visit neighbouring villages. It all seemed odd! On our return and my first day back at work, there was no one about. Normally the centre was a busy place with a continual flow of people passing through. The place was empty. The people I spoke to were crying! What's going on? It was very evident something had happened. The church had had a split! People were no longer there! They had left.

It was a painful time with many questions. All I felt led to do was continue to pray and fast another week and seek God's face. After work I was drawn to seek God and pray and wait quietly in His presence.

It was another learning curve. It is imperative that we hear from God for ourselves and not be persuaded by anyone wanting us to jump on their bandwagon. It's important we have God's mind and perspective on things and to make no decision till we know the mind and will of God for ourselves.

People spoke through their hurt and pain. It was a terrible time. God knew everything from every angle. Remaining close to Him was essential. In a situation like that what each person must do is keep their heart free from anger, bitterness, resentment and offence. Staying close to God is vital and keeping short accounts and mouths closed to gossiping is an absolute must. If we have a problem we need to speak to the person. If they do not listen then we take someone with us, in doing so we apply the Matthew 18:15-18 principle.

Waiting on Him is a choice we should make daily when facing a tough situation. Our aim should be to hear what God says before we leave offended or allow hurt or misunderstanding to wound us or our emotions to rule us. It should be God's voice we listen to not man's. We are called to love our brothers and sisters. Love is a choice. It always seemed stupid to me that we were part of the Body of Christ yet, thought nothing of taking an imaginary axe and chopping off an arm or a leg, thereby maiming the 'Body' we are part of, simply by gossiping. How self destructive can we be?

Continuing to forgive those who have betrayed us, wounded us or offended us is vitally important. Many people have not only been cut off from friends and members of the family of God but they have also ended up separated from Father God as a result. The enemy of our faith is a thief and a destroyer. The sad thing is, we allow him to continually attack us and we fail to use the authority we have been given to defeat his assignments against us.

Even the disciples had fall outs and differences of opinion as in Acts 15. The key thing is to hear from God for ourselves; hear what we are to do to obey Him and to keep in the centre of His will, loving like Jesus loves. It is also essential we are not swayed by other people's stories or feelings. Remembering we each have to give an account to God for our actions and responses helps us steer the right course and no one else can do it for us.

I learned another facet of 'suffering for the gospel's sake' in sharing the life of Jesus.

If we are followers of Jesus, it is guaranteed we will be ridiculed, rejected, betrayed, mocked, hated, left alone and isolated. This is the normal life of a follower of Jesus. Walking in His footsteps means we will all experience the things Jesus experienced, no matter what age we are! But the presence and love of God more than makes up for anything and everything we may painfully experience.

I was in charge of the Challenger bus team. Literally power and authority went to my head and I abused it. I side-stepped doing jobs I did not want to do. My attitude changed and I became very harsh and abrupt. We can sometimes forget that it's not only what we say that matters, but how it's said is just as important. People not only hear our words but they see our actions, expressions and behaviour too.

Jesus always had compassion and spoke graciously and truthfully to people. People were important to Him. He saw them as God's creation, fashioned to God's design. He spoke the truth very plainly. Matthew 23:27 says, "Woe to you, scribes and Pharisees, hypocrites! For you are like whitewashed tombs which indeed appear beautiful outwardly, but inside are full of dead men's bones and all uncleanness." That is certainly very straight!

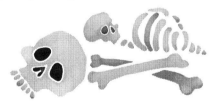

We do not have license to speak any way we want to people, which is yet another lesson to take on board and practise daily. I thank God He doesn't treat us as our sin deserves, or who could stand?

Many invitations would come in for me to speak at churches, youth groups, fellowships, women's groups and even prisons. Many times we are dropped in at the deep end. We have seconds to lean on Jesus and allow the Holy Spirit to carry us in the way of God, or we sink. This happened in Carstairs Prison one evening.

At the time it was a psychiatric hospital providing care and treatment in conditions of high security for around 140 patients from Scotland and Northern Ireland who needed to be detained in hospital under conditions of special security that can only be provided by the State Hospital.

The invitation stated that there could be up to fourteen men who would attend a meeting in a small room. I often took friends with me who could pray for me and the meeting. This evening especially demanded support and prayer cover.

When we arrived, my friends, Eileen, Val and I were shown into the gym hall instead of a small room. All forty men were there seated in a huge circle around the gym hall, with warders interspersed among them and officers also standing around the edge of the hall.

Talk about shaking knees! I jest not! Faces stared at me as I was asked to stand in the middle of this huge circle and speak. I felt totally exposed - because I was! At teaching college we were taught the maximum for a circle was eight or ten at the most.

'Help!' is one prayer I have used often. I had to really project my voice as I shared God's Word walking round and round the circle. It was hard trying to speak in the round! Talk about forcing myself not to be scared or put off by the looks on their stern faces as they stared at me. I mean the officers' faces!

Many men gave their lives to God that night. At the ministry time, there was one young man who came and asked for prayer for the voices in his head. He looked heavy with oppression and depression. Light was not evident in him. He prayed and asked Jesus to come into his life as his boss. My friend saw demons on his shoulders, speaking in his ears. We prayed and he was baptised in the Spirit. Then we prayed each demon off him and he was set free. His face shone. The evening ended with a fish supper at my Dad's after another adventure with Jesus.

About a year later, I was working in the Centre when a man came in asking to speak to me. Looking at him I decided I had not seen him before and therefore did not know him. He asked if I recognised him. Sorry. No I did not. He told me that after that night when he got prayer in Carstairs Prison, the voices in his head stopped totally. Such was the transformation in his behaviour that he was released. He had a new life with Jesus and went to a church in the village in which he was born. He came to say thanks! Truly all praise and glory goes to God. With God all things are possible.

God happens in the ordinary days of life. If we let Him! We are to be ready in season and out. That means we are to be ready anywhere and any time. If we walk in the Spirit then being ready is what life is all about.

Walking across a car park one night, I saw two men trying to get into a locked car. Their keys were locked inside. They had tried for ages borrowing lots of keys to try and see if one would open the door. None had.

"Can I help?" I asked.

I know prayer changes things. God can help anyone, anywhere with anything if we give Him a chance.

Oswald Chambers said we have to pray with our eyes on God not on the difficultly. So taking one of the keys I prayed over it and quickly stuck it in the lock and turned it without taking time to think. The door opened. "But we tried that key and it didn't work!" they said. But with God!

I had worked very hard for many months and started praying about a holiday. Once again I was exhausted. The fact I possessed only £8 did not worry me because I knew God could do anything!

One Saturday, a few weeks later a lady popped in on her way past my flat. She stood at the door and said she would give me money if I went abroad. Next day at church two friends who were engaged asked me if I would go on holiday with them as their 'chaperone.' But 'where' was the question?

As we sat in the coffee shop after church, Jacques the Swiss chap who was working with PWAMM in Scotland for some months, overheard our conversation and interrupted us by saying, "Come to Switzerland. I will phone my pastor and fix it". Literally at that exact moment our pastor walked past and Jacques asked him if he could phone home to Switzerland. "Use the office phone," he was told. Jacques came back and said that there was a lady back home who worked in an old folk's home for blind people. We could have two rooms there.

The next question was when?

Jacques had booked his ticket home from London months ago. Before we knew it we had the dates fixed. How amazing is God? It was now September and we had decided we were going to Switzerland. I then received four belated birthday cards containing cheques and letters apologising for forgetting my birthday earlier in the month. I had pocket money. Although my friends were going for two weeks, I decided to stay an extra week.

While standing in the queue at London airport to book in, a man passed by me and pressed something into my hand. I nearly fainted and danced with joy because when I looked it was a £100 pound note!

We caught the flight after Jacques and when his friend met him at the airport in a minibus, we got picked up too. We went to Ecublens near Lausanne in Switzerland. We all got on really well and visited Jacques' church. We met his pastor and his pastor's wife and friends. The pace of life in Switzerland was exceptionally different from that of Perth. It was slow!

The pastor shared a story in which he had been involved. He had a mighty deliverance session with someone, seeing them being totally set free. The newspapers and TV got a hold of this and as far as the world was concerned, they gave him and his church some 'bad' publicity. However, the pastor said it was free advertising for Jesus. After this, he received phone calls from people from all over Switzerland who asked him for healing and deliverance. At that time not too many pastors could pray that way for people.

We enjoyed our holiday greatly. Denise, with whom we were staying, said we had to see Gruyère cows. After a bus journey up the really steep side of a very high mountain we arrived at the coffee shop. She settled us in and ordered us each a scone and milk. I wanted to opt out as the thought of eating a scone with milk certainly did not appeal to me. However, she insisted. And when it came the milk was actually cream. The milk was so thick it looked like our cream! It was absolutely lovely.

We did the usual tourist things, enjoying sightseeing and, of course, the sun. One day we went to a park beside a lake. There were some guys playing football and my friend joined in. He brought back a young seven year old boy and we shared our picnic with him. He told us that his mother and father were separated. His father worked in Australia and his mum and he lived in the hotel nearby. He was a lovely wee boy and clever too; he spoke three languages. We shared the good news with him and he thought it was "Good News" and responded to Jesus by faith. He also spoke in his fourth language. Tongues! He was baptised in the Holy Spirit.

After he went home, I went for a walk, praising and thanking God for another divine appointment. I sat enjoying the lovely day when I suddenly had a sense of 'go back now' to my friends. Walking along the path I saw my friend run towards me and she filled me in. The wee boy's mother had come looking for us because she wanted to know what had happened to her son. It's easy to think the worst first! Was she going to have it out with us? Why is it so difficult for us to assume the best first and not the worst?

We shared the gospel message with her. She was a much wounded, hurt and rejected woman. Her husband had left her for a younger woman and she was shocked. Her whole life was in a complete state of 'all change'.

We shared how it was in her best interest to forgive her husband and his girlfriend and to hand them over to God. After asking all her questions, she realised she needed the love and forgiveness of a Saviour who died for her sins. She became born again, baptised in the Holy Spirit and set free from rejection, pain and heartbreak. She left us a lighter, brighter woman. God knows the rest of her story as He does ours.

After my friends went home to Scotland I still had another week. I had decided that I wanted to seek God. I praised and worshipped God. I prayed in the Spirit for hours a day. I did a study on Deborah, the only woman Judge mentioned in the Bible. I sought God to know Him more. I waited on Him.

During this week I believed I heard God say my younger sister would have another baby. I knew that she did not want another baby, so I left it with God. God spoke clearly and I heard. I knew I was to be obedient to what He showed me to do during this time.

Two friends were planning a holiday and I felt I had to phone home to share a word God gave me for them. The call came at just the right time. God saved them from an open door the enemy was planning to use.

A picture was given to me. I saw myself walk from the back of my church to the platform and I felt the power of God's anointing touch my mouth to enable me to speak. Again I left it all with God.

One afternoon He said I was to go up to the top of the mountain in front of the old folk's home. There was a steep path up each side of the mountain. I walked up the path nearest to where I was staying. At the top there was a levelled area with another path opposite the one I had walked up. At the edge were huge boulders where people could sit to enjoy the view, which was what I did.

The tops of all the pointed mountains around me went right through the clouds. It was beautiful. The mountains were huge and stable and they loomed loftily in front of me as the verse from Isaiah 54:10 came to mind. "For the mountains shall depart and the hills be removed, but My kindness shall not depart from you, nor shall My covenant of peace be removed," says the Lord, who has mercy on you.

In a split moment of time I had a very simple revelation. How hard or impossible would it be for these huge mountains to be shaken, perhaps wobble like jelly and be removed? And God was saying His unfailing love for me would not be shaken nor His covenant of peace be removed. In that sudden moment I knew, but I knew the reality of God's everlasting Covenant with me and His love for me. It was awesome.

As I sat there bowled over by His unfailing love for me, I caught sight of a woman probably in her late sixties, walking up the path. She looked tired and weary. The Holy Spirit said, "She is going to come and sit next to you. She needs to be saved and healed." Sure enough she sat on the huge boulder next to me. We smiled at each other. We looked at the scenery. She spoke French as she said, "Bonjour." It was lovely to see how God brought back French vocabulary I had learned years ago. She shared her story. She came from Spain to Switzerland about thirty years ago. She met and married her husband but now that he had passed away she was lonely. As a Roman Catholic she knew about Jesus but did not know Him. When I shared how much God loved her and gave Jesus for her, she said she knew this but when I shared about meeting Jesus as Lord she cried. If I said something really badly in French, and she did not understand, the Holy Spirit showed me a different way of saying it with words I could remember. She nodded. She wanted to ask Jesus to forgive her for her sin, to thank Him for dying for her and she asked Him into her heart. After praying she sighed, saying, "Merci Monsieur, Merci Monsieur" over and over and over again. She then was baptised in the Spirit. Just after this we heard voices approaching from the other path behind us. It was Jacque's pastor's wife and granddaughter. What amazing timing and it was so lovely to see them.

I was about to introduce the two ladies but had no need to because when the Spanish woman first came to Switzerland she had met the pastor's wife who had encouraged her to come to her husband's church. The Spanish woman had declined. Now after all this time she was ecstatic to see her. I shared how she had cancer and so we prayed for her healing. The two older women walked down the path together chatting happily. I love it when a plan of God comes together.

It was time to return home.

The first place I went to was church. I was asked to share about my time in Switzerland. It was amazing knowing the Holy Spirit was speaking through me. It was just like I had seen in the vision.

Then I went to see my father. As I was about to turn into my father's driveway, I saw my sister, her young son on a bike and the next door neighbour walking up the road. My nephew cycled ahead excitedly and then letting his bike fall to the ground, rushed up to hug me, repeating, "My mum's getting a baby in the summer."

It was encouraging to know I had heard from God after all, even though at that time she had not particularly planned to have another baby. But later she said that she could not imagine life without her daughter.

A woman I knew who worked in a Christian establishment doing all kinds of jobs, was really down about what was happening at her place of work. It was an hour's journey there and it was late when I arrived. No one else was in that night. We chatted, prayed, and then it was time for me to go. As I walked along the corridor towards the front door, my feet stuck like glue and I could not take another step. At which time I also started speaking loudly in tongues or roaring to be more precise. Words poured out of my mouth which were not mine! 'God was going to reveal hidden things and grant justice for the oppressed in that place.' This was the first time I had ever prophesied.

A short while later it was discovered that finances were being misappropriated and the person responsible was discovered and removed. God knows everything that goes on behind the scenes. No one ever pulls the wool over His eyes. We can truly trust Him with every area of our lives and in the right way, at the right time, He brings justice to us.

God knows best. Always!

Many plans, purposes, timings, questions and God knows each one.

Our church in Perth had a Sunday evening service in Edinburgh. One night there was a special speaker, Keith Mason. The praise and worship was really anointed. Talk about being lost in worship. I did not stay in the room. I literally visited heaven! No one was around me, everyone in the room vanished. I was conscious of an extremely bright light. It was brilliant white and I could not look at it. There was a throne in the midst of the light. I was awestruck! I did not fully understand what was happening at the time.

The next thing I knew was the brilliant light exposed my pain. It shone in the dark hidden recesses of my heart exposing my deepest, darkest secret just like when the sun shines exposing layers of dust. Everywhere dust, dust, and even more dust for the whole neighbourhood to see! I was shocked. The pain rushed from its hidden place deep within me and caused me to relive the experiences. I had been an expert at suppressing the memories which were now being brought to the surface. Hysterical crying was heard. It was me! Friends sitting around asked me what was wrong. I brushed them away. What a state I was in!

The speaker came up and said God had shown him what was wrong with me. An appointment was arranged for me to go to him one afternoon for prayer, with two of the women from church.

God uses many different ways to expose what is hidden in us. It could be a difference of opinion with someone or pressure brought about by a prescribed set of circumstances. A person with cancer does not go to a surgeon for him to put a plaster on the cancer. Instead the skilled surgeon uses his sharp scalpel and cuts it out totally. Unless he removes the cancer completely, it can grow bigger and spread to healthy areas causing even more damage and pain and eventually it can lead to death.

God knows exactly how to remove the 'death-causing thing' in us. An operation is not a particularly pleasant experience but it is absolutely vital to save our lives. Always there is healing after the pain.

Many people are walking about with various 'diseases' that only God can remove skilfully and bring healing to their lives. But before healing there must be a bringing of the thing into the light. It is a fearful thing to do but it enables it to be dealt with first, roots killed and then healing enjoyed.

The speaker prayed for my dark secret to be removed and for me to be healed. It was not exactly a pleasant experience as it was painful facing the memories of sexual abuse.

Before I could receive my healing I had to forgive the person involved. Unforgiveness and bitterness stop the complete work being done. The choice was made, forgiveness given and healing experienced.

He explained that when we experience shocking and painful things, unclean spirits can come in and cause us problems like feelings of shame, revulsion, heartbreak to name a few. He prayed against the unclean spirits and commanded them to go in Jesus' name. The blood of Jesus was prayed over me and I experienced the power that was in the blood and in the name of Jesus. Tiredness engulfed me but only after I had experienced deliverance and freedom.

I was set free at exactly the right time on God's timetable. Why now and not previously? If I am yielded to Him He knows what is in me, because He sees everything about my life, past, present and future. As He is God, He knows when it is time to deal with things, even if we would rather keep them hidden and out of sight.

Before this I had never experienced prayer touch my life so powerfully. I was free and I knew it. I was clean and I loved it. I was healed and I enjoyed it. This was my first deliverance experience. There would be more to come. After having received my freedom, I then found that I met so many people, both men and women, who had experienced sexual abuse. Having been shown how to pray for their healing and deliverance, it enabled me to see them come into freedom. Many people, many stories, many places, much glory to God.

Glory to God!

God's Presence
and Power
in the Communities

The vision of PWAMM was then and is now to take the power and presence of God into the communities of Scotland. People in churches and fellowships all over Scotland would faithfully pray every day for God to move on the streets, on the bus and in communities. One important prayer we believed on a daily basis was "send Your divine appointments Lord". We would expect His 'divine appointments' to come onto the bus, or pass by the bus daily. They came in many shapes, sizes, ages and from all different backgrounds.

One day a lady came on board and spoke about her need of healing. She had had a knot like pain in her stomach for over a year. The doctors did a lot of tests and could not find a medical cause. She had just returned that day from an appointment with her consultant but there was still no answer to her problem and the pain persisted. She assured us the pain was real and not a figment of her imagination, as had been suggested. She was a Christian already. She went to church and she read her Bible but she was in pain. As I listened to her I was praying quietly in the Spirit and I heard, "Ask her with whom she is bitter?" So I did. At that point her husband said he had to go and he went downstairs.

She immediately started to angrily answer the question recounting a story about a member of her family. Bitterness, yes, also rage, unforgiveness, resentment, hatred and short of murder, she drew breath. God had hit the nail on the head. He knows the roots of all our problems. He knows the questions to ask to release the torment of pain. He knows everything about us: where we have been, where we are now and how we are, and where we are going.

As she spoke, the knot like pain in her stomach increased. She cried out. An explanation of forgiveness followed. In order to receive forgiveness of our sins, we are commanded to forgive others or God won't forgive us. The Bible tells us in Matthew 6:14-15 "For if you forgive men their trespasses, your heavenly Father will also forgive you. But if you do not forgive men their trespasses, neither will your Father forgive your trespasses".

Forgiveness heals spiritual wounds, brings peace and healing which only God can give. Initially she refused to forgive because she hated the person for the deep hurt caused and did not feel she could forgive. After prayer she was told forgiveness is a choice; it's not a feeling. We forgive because we are commanded to, so in obedience to God's Word she finally prayed and asked Jesus to help her to be willing to forgive with His forgiveness and then she chose to forgive them. The spirit of bitterness was evicted and she felt the knot in her stomach unravel and go fully. Peace flooded her and she was made well.

The Challenger bus team were asked to visit a church outside Glasgow. The church was meeting in a school. The team were busy working with the children and we were expecting an influx of children at the Sunday morning service. We were well prepared, however no children turned up! We went to the evening service where we were expecting adults but a whole bunch of children turned up and we were not prepared. We had nothing with us except our Bibles and the Holy Spirit. The pastor asked us to take the children to another room because they were being a bit disruptive in the hall at the beginning of the service.

The school janitor showed us a music room at the end of a long corridor, where we could do something with the children. Disruptive children in a music room full of instruments! Please God, help! I felt like the Pied Piper of Hamelin walking down the corridor followed by a line of noisy children, with Val the other team member at the end of the line.

I was praying furiously in tongues. The religious church is afraid of the Baptism of the Holy Spirit. The enemy hates the spiritual language. Paul wrote and spoke a lot about speaking in tongues. 1 Corinthians 14:18, "I thank my God I speak with tongues more than you all".

The early church in Acts 2:4 spoke in tongues as an initial sign of baptism of the Holy Spirit. Paul encouraged the Corinthian Christians to speak with other tongues in their worship to God. He also encouraged them to speak in tongues in their individual prayer lives as a means of building themselves up in their 'spirit-man' as in 1 Corinthians 14:14. When we speak in tongues we are talking to God by divine, supernatural means. It also helps us to be continually aware of the Holy Spirit's presence. It's a Spirit-led praying and it helps us to trust God. Trusting God was what we were doing as we walked along that corridor.

I didn't know what to do. But He does and did. I entered the music room and spoke out loud in tongues as I smiled at each child pointing to a chair expecting each child to sit down, which they did. As they all sat down, they asked each other, "What's she saying?" with quizzical looks on their surprised faces.

"Does anyone know what language I'm speaking?" I asked.

"French, German, Dutch," came their suggestions.

"Good guesses, but no!"

Let's sing! It got their attention, they were quiet. They sat quietly and participated really well and ignored all the instruments! We sang choruses, told a Bible story, had a quiz, shared testimony and prayed. Time was up! It was an ordered time, a good time, and chaos was not evident after all! God is so good. All we need is Jesus. He is our vital necessity at all times.

During another mission the bus was parked beside a river. It was a nice sunny day and the bus was busy with a steady flow of people. The bus raised curiosity wherever it went. Out of the corner of my eye I noticed a young woman who stood afar off watching the bus. There was darkness, nervousness and a fear that emanated from her!

During the day I prayed, "Lord let the girl overcome her fear, bring her and touch her please." In the afternoon she did come on board although rather hesitantly and very nervously.

She sat upstairs and told her story. During an ouija board session she was freaked out beyond belief at what happened. She breathed in and believed a spirit of a woman entered her. She was changed from that point on. A severe rage and anger took hold of her. She felt helpless. She would have no control over her reactions. Once when her boyfriend read the Bible, as he was seeking God, she flew into a rage and attacked him. He ran and locked himself in the toilet for protection and safety.

She responded in faith to the gospel and was baptised in the Spirit. When Graeme and I started to pray for her and told the evil spirit to leave, it spoke through her in an angry, strong voice, "No. This is my home!"

People are ignorant of the dangers they open themselves up to when they dabble with the supernatural world of the occult. Having participated in that myself I knew from first-hand experience.

However, the power of God is more powerful than the power of Satan. The girl was set free and filled with peace and joy.

The Bible says that God goes before us. Things that hurt and wound us, confuse us or even upset us are all already known to God and there is nothing we can do or say that will ever surprise Him or shock Him or make Him not love us or accept us. He knows us intimately and loves us completely and eternally.

I learned quickly that when a bus goes on a mission, it is not always the strangers who wander aboard that are our divine appointments. It was sometimes the church team or even the pastors or ministers who were in God's eyesight. It was lovely to see them encouraged and strengthened. Simply having a listening ear and a willingness to pray always helped them. Prayer does change things. Always!

One morning the owner of the house where we were staying, opened his mail and his countenance changed. Something was wrong. You can't make someone tell you anything, but you can pray that they decide to share their problem. Later on he did. He had received a poison-pen letter. The content hurt him and he wished he had the opportunity to speak directly to the anonymous writer. We prayed about the letter and especially for the person who sent it.

On the bus later that night, a mother came to collect her child. It was apparent something was disturbing her. Praying in the Spirit quietly under my breath, we started to speak about regrets that we have. This was the key to opening up her biggest regret; the regret of sending a letter. Salvation followed, forgiveness experienced and peace received. She left knowing she had to speak to someone urgently.

The bus team members were excellent. All had different skills and talents. All worked really hard. One of the guys in the church, a recent convert, asked if he could come on a mission. He was willing to do anything, serve tea, hand out tracts just simply do anything. He was invited on the next mission and invited passers-by on board the bus as he had a bright, sunny, personality and a smiley face.

There was a homeless person who kept passing the bus and declined each invitation issued to come on board. He became more inebriated as the day went on, and swore at everyone as he passed by.

Our new team member encouraged him aboard. He eventually came. The visitor wanted to know why his face shone. "Jesus" was his reply. After the guys chatted to him, it was decided he needed a shower, some clean clothes and food. He was taken to a home nearby and taken care of, to return later to the bus. He gave his life to Christ. As he was going off the bus our hearts were touched. Where would he go, back to the fields and streets to live? No!

Mr 'Smiley' and his wife looked at each other and then invited him home with them to live with their family. He slept in their living room for months and was loved and cared for. Truly he had a new life. When he got on his feet he moved on, to return about a year later, unrecognisable. He was amazing. God was putting his life back together.

There were occasions, however, when there were complaints. I remember a letter was sent and a minister asked to speak to me as he did not like the message of the bus. He was a retired minister of a certain denomination. He agreed with the message of salvation but struggled with the Holy Spirit. I met him to discuss his objections. We looked at what the Word of God said. The problem was that he had a gap between his knowledge and experience. Was he open to receiving? He would think about it. He bumped into me a few years later and told me that he was baptised in the Spirit later on at a conference he had gone to in England. He understood finally what it was all about. He blessed the work of the bus.

On another mission in Dumfries, a local church elder came on board the bus. Initially he quite liked the idea of the bus. Unfortunately that changed when he was asked if he had a personal relationship with Jesus. He became quite angry and blurted out that this was not necessary. The most important thing was going to church. How many people believe in church yet do not believe that Jesus is the way, the truth and the life and that no one goes to the Father except through Him? (John 14: 6.) He stormed off the bus. We prayed God would show him the truth.

The next time the bus visited that area, the elder came back to speak to me. He shared truthfully that he had left annoyed by the last question he was asked. He started to read and study the word of God for himself. He found out that Jesus Himself said he needed to be born again. So he was. He came back to thank us for stirring him up to search the truth for himself. Now he was a born again believer. This time when he was on the bus he was also baptised in the Holy Spirit. No resistance stopped him from receiving this time as he saw the truth clearly written in the Bible.

God says in Isaiah 28:10 " for precept must be upon precept, precept upon precept, line upon line, line upon line, here a little, there a little." God spoon feeds us a bit at a time and knows when we are ready for the next spoonful.

Some missions saw God do miracles of healing. On one mission, Tom, one of the team, prayed for a man's finger which had nerve damage causing stiffness and numbness. One prayer and it was completely healed.

On another mission to Rothesay a teenage pupil from the local school came on the bus and one of the team prayed for his hand which was broken. He too was healed. The news spread around the secondary school. The last day of that mission, we had to speak at a lunch time Scripture Union group meeting. Guess who turned up to share his healing story? The healed teenager of course! He was there sharing testimony. But there was an unexpected guest too. The depute headmaster was curious to know what this was all about. He sat up the back of the class listening attentively. It was later discovered his daughter, Lesley, was a Christian and he had heard other testimonies but had not really believed. There was no disputing the evidence before him. The boy's hand was healed.

On that same mission we were staying with the pastor and his wife and family. After the morning service, someone had gone back early to put on the lunch. When we got back, it was discovered that the huge pot of potatoes, for about twelve people, had been forgotten. A pot that size would take ages to boil never mind cook. However, we have an amazing God with whom all things are possible. Liz, the pastor's wife, and I agreed in prayer, that they would be ready to eat after our soup. When we were ready to dish up those potatoes, they were cooked perfectly! A miracle indeed!

Divine appointments weren't only met on the bus. Some friends were staying with me one weekend in my one-bed roomed flat because there was a conference on. At the end of the night, as we were driving down to my flat we saw four ladies with backpacks walk past. It was a dreadfully rainy night, and they were all really soaked. It was around midnight. They jumped at the chance of staying in a flat. What are four more bodies staying over? They were from Belgium and had put up their tent in the South Inch Park in front of my flat but had been annoyed by a gang of teenagers. They felt they needed to move on for safety's sake. We had a great time chatting and sharing and eating and drinking warm drinks, then lying like sardines in sleeping bags!

Some say you never know what a day holds but we can say we know Who holds each day. Many people, many stories, many divine appointments and much glory to God.

On another occasion I was going home when I met a young girl walking along the road. I asked if she would like a lift. It turned out she was a young Christian girl who was hurting. We spoke and we prayed. Encouragement and prayer are so necessary for all of us and we need to be on the alert to notice when those around us need a comforting arm, a shoulder to cry on, a hand to hold, a listening ear or a chance to speak, and prayers to be said. We need to guard against having our eyes so much on self that we miss those in need around us.

A few years later when at lunch in a pastor's house in walked his son and daughter in law. We were introduced. The daughter-in-law said that she already knew me. I did not recognise her. She said I had given her a lift and a prayer one day and that God had turned her life around. We don't always get to hear, this side of heaven, what happens after we meet someone but we look forward to finding out one day.

I visited a church with a colleague some years ago. A man in a suit came up and spoke to me. Again I did not recognise him as a former drug addict who got saved on the bus. Another testimony of God taking His power and presence to the communities of Scotland and touching lives in the process. Many Christians were encouraged, challenged, and stirred up, encountering the Jesus who is still the same as He was long ago. Jesus is the same yesterday, today, and forever. (Hebrews 13:8)

Many unsaved people encountered Jesus on the streets and on the Challenger bus. Many responded to the Good News with open hearts, repenting of their sins and receiving Jesus as their Lord and Saviour. They left to begin and enjoy a new life.

However, many people did not respond to the love Jesus showed them as He died on Calvary for their sins to be forgiven. The amazing thing about God is, that He still loves them perfectly with the same love as He has for Jesus. Each of us has the free will to choose Jesus or reject Him.

Praise God for the many lives which have been transformed by His love. What an amazing time we have to look forward to when we all meet up in heaven. I cannot wait!

Transition
out of Perth

As Christians we are in a constant state of transition and change. The Bible talks about being changed from one degree of glory to another. The dictionary says transition means change; a passage or period of time from one stage to another. Amazing stories in the Word of God teach us about the nature and character of God and His ways towards His people. We may change but one thing we are guaranteed is that God never changes.

I read about how God brought the Israelites out of Egypt that He might bring them into the Promised Land. What I was reading in Exodus was happening to me in Perth. Scriptures like Deuteronomy 32:11-12, "As an eagle stirs up its nest, hovers over its young, spreading out its wings, taking them up, carrying them on its wings, so the Lord alone led him," and Joshua 3:4 "that you may know the way by which you must go, for you have not passed this way before".

Although I kept reading about God saying, "Behold, I will do a new thing," in Isaiah 43:19 "Now it shall spring forth; shall you not know it? I will even make a road in the wilderness and rivers in the desert". I was comfortable and very happy where I was. I had no intention of moving, so swept God's words under the carpet.

God gives us a choice. He wants us to hear and obey. Effectively what I was doing was not listening and disobeying.

Things started ruining my peace and upsetting my comfort. The petrol in my car was stolen as thieves burst my tank. Forgiving those who sin against us is not always easy but God commands us to. The following week my car window was smashed. How many times are we meant to forgive? More than we would like! Seventy times seven says Jesus! At the end of the day my purse was hit hard financially.

During this time I became ill. God knows best how to stir up our nest!

My neighbours started to complain about me. The fact that I got on well with all of them while I had lived there for ten years, did not count. Letters were written to the council complaining about the people I had visiting. One person had a backpack on! Can you imagine the horror of it?

Finally a council official visited me at 8.30am in the morning carrying a dossier on me. I couldn't believe how thick it was with all my neighbours' letters of complaint. I was given a warning not to have as many people visiting.

I told myself to keep forgiving or else bitterness and resentment would build up quickly poisoning my mind and heart and affecting my walk with God.

During this time, work changed too. God has His ways of disconnecting us during our transition period.

To move on, we have to let go. He shakes the familiar, the comfortable, the peaceful and we can either react or respond. It's down to a choice again. God showed me the difference between reacting and responding. Reacting is fighting what is happening and complaining about what takes place. Reacting can cause us to see the hand of man. However, responding is allowing God to do what He wants without reacting in our flesh or soul realm.

If God works in us both to will and to do His good pleasure as it says in Philippians 2:13, we must realise good is the enemy of better and ultimately better is the enemy of best.

It is not pleasant being under the pruning hand of Almighty God, no matter how essential it is. Unless He prunes us we cannot bear much more fruit. (John 15) Pruning can come in many shapes and sizes but remember it is our Father who knows what is in us and what needs to be pruned. We may kick, shout, cry, moan and complain but the pruning process is in the hand of God and He knows how long it will take to deal with the hidden sin and wrong attitudes deep inside us, which we, for the most part, are ignorant of or are unwilling to deal with.

God uses many things in the pruning process; misunderstandings, betrayals, offences, sickness, financial problems and disagreements are just a few of His ways. Each time He looks for maturity. Do we face the fiery trials with faith, trust, love, forgiveness, mercy and repentance? Do we grow in the knowledge of our God during such trials, or do we shrink away from His love, grace and mercy, and slip into darkness by allowing unforgiveness, bitterness, anger or hatred to take root in our hearts? Arthur Burt from Wales said, "If you feel far from God, guess who moved?".

During my transition time I struggled with my emotions. My head knew what I should do and finally my heart got the enabling grace to do it. Many a time I drove up a hill praying, praising and giving thanks through floods of tears. For years I had collected memorial stones from the various trials and tests I had gone through. Some stones were small and beautiful, others were big and ugly, some were huge and heavy. Each carried a memory of the experience I went through, reminding me of the pain, the lessons learned and always the faithfulness of God to carry me through. They used to sit in full view in a wooden tray at the side of my fireplace, reminding me that He promised never to leave me or forsake me.

At least I had learned something over my years as a Christian, instead of dwelling on the actions of others, to focus instead on my Father in heaven. It was a painful and difficult time but I was not on my own..

One weekend I went to Glentrool village to stay with my friend Morag. I journeyed through hills and valleys on my way, by the back road, to my friend's house. I stopped when I got to the top of the mountain where it levelled out; I admired the spectacular view. It was a lovely sunny day and the scenery ministered to my soul. As no one was about I started to praise God at the top of my voice. It was amazing. I felt strengthened and loved by my Father in heaven. I cried out to Him asking Him what was happening to me.

He simply said, "I AM" God was behind 'all this'.

Yielding to change is what we must do when it is God who is orchestrating the change. Embracing change is really hard but it is not impossible especially when He gives great grace.

At church one Sunday a few weeks later, an Irish visitor, whom I had never seen before, came to me at the end of the service. He said that God was pleased because I had chosen to exercise my will and forgive. "It doesn't matter if it's not reciprocated," he went on to say.

We cannot make anyone forgive us nor can we make anyone speak to us or discuss matters. We are each responsible for our own hearts, and the actions and decisions we make. We will face our Maker in the end. He knows everything about every situation we have ever faced. We cannot fool our Father in heaven. He knows absolutely everything about our lives.

We, however, see things mostly from our perspective. God sees both sides at the same time and is familiar with every word spoken, every decision made, every thought and attitude expressed, whether verbally or internally.

God had finally got my attention. I was willing to listen and obey. It didn't matter what anyone thought. The key issue was, what did God think?

The final nail in my cross at this time was Acts 5:29. "We ought to obey God rather than men."

What exactly was God asking me to do? He wanted me to leave Perth and go back to my father's house. This did not make sense but I was finally willing, although one more confirmation would be good!

I had a dental appointment and while sitting quietly in the waiting room, a Baptist lady I knew, came in, smiled at me and sat down opposite me. She then moved beside me and started singing quietly in my ear, "One more step along the world I go, from the old things to the new, keep me travelling along with You."

How amazing was her obedience in God making really clear His will to me.

The morning I wrote my resignation letter I prayed again for one final confirmation. As my pen was poised over the blank sheet of paper, the phone went. A friend in a Baptist Church in Selkirk, said she had a very clear picture of me. I was dressed in a coat, carrying two suitcases walking out of a red sandstone building. She wanted to know what was going on.

Many disagreed with my obedience to God in leaving work and Perth; but God always confirms His Word. The night I left PWAMM, I had made a long standing arrangement to go to an FGB meeting in Dunfermline. The speaker that night did not know me but of course God did. The speaker said that I had been obedient to God's will for my life and that God would lead me in my journey of faith one step at a time. This was another confirming, encouraging word. So I left my work in Perth. However, I did not go back to my Dad's for several months. During this time I realised that partial obedience was really disobedience. So arrangements were made to move back home to Newarthill.

I had no money to move but I received a cheque in the post for the exact amount needed to hire a van to move my belongings. Help was given to pack the van in Perth and at my Dad's a pastor and his two sons were waiting to help me unload the van. Once again the Lord undertook.

My father welcomed me with open arms. I was blessed in so many ways. I got time to play with my niece and nephew and catch up with friends and have a good rest.

One day while playing with my four year old niece in my father's back garden, I suddenly realised that she was running around with one hand up in the air.

"What are you doing with your hand up?" I asked. She brought her hand down to show me a melted chocolate biscuit. "He's not getting this one!" she declared emphatically. 'He' being my father's dog! He had previously snatched two biscuits very craftily out of her hand. No more! She had learned that if she kept her biscuit at dog level, he enjoyed more than she!

How often do we allow the enemy to snatch something from us, perhaps our joy, our peace, or a Scriptural truth? The first time we can say we were taken by surprise, the second time we may not have been prepared. But we can all learn from a little child! My niece, all of four, learned quickly. She took precautions. The dog could snatch the biscuit if she held it down low, but not if he could not reach it! How simple is that? The church knows there is nothing new under the sun. The enemy's strategies do not change. He likes to cause worry and anxiety by sowing negative thoughts into our minds, next we lose our peace and joy. Truly God knows we are to take captive every thought and make it obedient to Christ. What do we need to do to make sure the enemy is stopped in his tracks? What do we need to do to give him no space in our thoughts or lives? Use the authority we have and follow God's instructions in His Word. We must reject Satan's lies the moment they come to our mind or are heard in our ears.

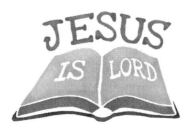

My transition through this wilderness time made me realise that God is Lord. Everything seemed to be out of control but I absolutely knew He was in control. Everything felt strange. I felt strange. I didn't feel a part of anything. I missed my Christian family and work in Perth. However, I had special friends who prayed faithfully and supported me. God made sure my life was not full of distractions. He knew I needed to focus on Him at this time. It was like being pulled away from the world and looking closely at what was buried deep inside me and receiving prayer and ministry to deal with issues that were being brought to the surface.

The old life was gone and I really wasn't sure what was next; where I was supposed to be or what I was meant to do? I knew, however, that God did.

When you think of it, a wilderness isn't like a busy shopping centre. It's usually a hot, unshaded expanse of land where feeling alone and lost is normal. Jesus was led by the Spirit into the wilderness and if we are followers of Jesus then we too will be led into the wilderness and will experience it just as Jesus did. It's about being tested. God sets the test.

We may ask, as I did, "What's happening to me?" I didn't get an answer to that question for a long time. When He said, "I AM" it made sense to stop wrestling with the circumstances and let go and let God!

In the wilderness we are hidden from public view. I came to realise that my identity had been in my title.

To say simply in response to who I was when I went to churches or meetings, my reply was "May Dow." Gone were the titles I had grown accustomed to. It was back to basics and not before time. Simply put, God showed me once again that my pride was a stench in His nostrils.

A common error is to believe we must "do" for God to love us. Learning afresh that we are loved unconditionally all the time and it has absolutely nothing to do with our performance was very humbling and once again refreshing.

It was hard "just being me." No expectations, no levels to attain. I was already in Christ and seated in the heavenly realms with Him. I was already loved by God with the same love He had for Jesus. God so loved me that He lavished His love on me, May Dow. I was unique and special to my Father in heaven. I was blown away.

The enemy wants us to move in the flesh and soul realm. All the while God wants to get us to simply yield; submit and give in to Him. Just as in a wilderness you think you see water in an oasis, your mind plays tricks on you. The enemy tries to get us to believe we have no faith, or we have made a mistake and a whole lot more. It's a war against who we are, what we believe and the decisions we make. One thing for sure, the wilderness is not easy or enjoyable and certainly not fun! However, it is necessary, precious, unforgettable and significant. Why? It is part of His plan. If the Holy Spirit led Jesus into the wilderness, we can be sure He will lead us there too. We are, after all, His followers!

We learn that God uses some tough lessons to teach us more of His ways; the ways of the cross. I had never before seen some 'hard' Scripture verses like Psalms 66:11. "You brought us into the net; you laid affliction on our backs". This was a side of God I was learning about in the fiery trial. I cannot say it was a beautiful, peaceful and lovely experience, but it was God teaching me facets of His holy character.

Someone once said that everything in our Christian life is like a bunch of roses. We discover quickly and painfully that roses have thorns! However, after the wilderness, we come out into the Promised Land in God's time for God's purpose and we are filled with power.

During this interesting time some friends from Peterhead blessed me with a tour of the Holy Land. It was an incredible experience. I visited Jerusalem, Nazareth, Bethlehem, Caesarea, Mount Carmel, the Sea of Galilee, Jericho and Ein Gedi, Qumran and Masada to name but a few places. Seeing the environment and reading the stories that took place there brought a whole new perspective to the Bible I had not imagined. It impacted me greatly. I read the Bible with better understanding. I had seen the terrain, the people, the places and it brought out a new dimension of the Word in relation to the land of Israel. I so wanted to go back one day.

My heavenly Father knows what we need when we need it. His aim is always for us to really know Him, trust Him, believe Him and enjoy Him. Even in the midst of trials and wilderness times, and going through transition, we need never doubt His love for us nor forget that He is always with us. I love the fact that, though I may not always know the way ahead, my task is to simply follow the steps my Father shows me. He has gone ahead and yet He goes with me every step of the yellow brick road I walk.

New Life in Paisley and Beyond!

Habakkuk 2:3 says, *"For the vision is yet for an appointed time; but at the end it will speak, and it will not lie. Though it tarries, wait for it; because it will surely come, it will not tarry."*

God may give us a word, a vision or a promise and in our hearts we may wish it would manifest right away. God's time, however, is not our time.

The Bible says in 2 Peter 3:8 *"But, beloved, do not forget this one thing, that with the Lord one day is as a thousand years, and a thousand years as one day."*

Looking back things can seem as if they happened only yesterday and looking forward they seem to take forever to come.

When I first moved to Perth, I loved my work. I was completely satisfied and enjoyed watching what God did. Suddenly within one week three Scripture Union prayer supporters phoned me or wrote to me to say that I had to be open for God giving me a husband. To be honest I did not particularly want a husband; however, I did ask God to make me open.

Shortly after this I was going to a prayer meeting one night. On the way there I felt that if I was asked for a personal prayer request, then I would ask if they could pray for a husband for me. I thought this was being open for a husband.

After the prayer meeting, it was time for a cup of tea and no one asked me if I wanted prayer. All of a sudden the hostess said, "Ladies, stop! We haven't asked if May wants prayer". The cups of tea were left. They started praying for me, for a husband.

Over the years God said the following things regarding my husband; if I was obedient, suddenly I would meet him; that he would have worked abroad; that I would know him but not know him (that was a conundrum God would solve) and that we would get married in November; also that I would see why things were the way they were.

However, it would be twelve years before I met him! I was staying with my father for nearly a year after I left Perth and went to a small Christian Fellowship in St Catherine's in Argyll. It was July 27th, a beautiful sunny Sunday as I drove the hour and half there. As usual I had a great time praying and praising God and I said, "Lord when is my husband coming? It's been twelve years".

Back came the reply, "If you are obedient, suddenly I will do it!" I had heard that before!

After the service I went to the pastors' home for lunch. Later on that afternoon I returned home, admiring the stunning scenery going over the Rest and be Thankful road making my way towards Tarbet. As I was passing a former church then called The Black Sheep Restaurant and Gift Shop I heard, "Turn in here now!" I was nearly past the entrance, so I made a very quick and sudden turn to the left and entered the car park.

Why was I here? I really did not know other than God had said go in. So I decided I would go and have a look. When I was walking back to my car I saw an old lady with a stick walking towards me. "Speak to her," the Holy Spirit said.

"Oh it's a lovely evening isn't it?" I blurted out. She gave me an unwelcome look and asked in a crisp voice with a cold glare on her surprised face, "Are you speaking to me?"

We started talking about the lovely weather and got on to the gospel. She needed salvation and healing. I told her about a healing meeting each Saturday in Glasgow. I said I would write to her with the time and address. At that point a man joined us, her son Campbell. As I wrote her address she asked me where I lived. I told her a wee village near Motherwell that would probably be unknown to her.

"Newarthill! Why, my aunt Mary stays there!" she declared surprised.

"Who is that?" I enquired.

Mrs Mary Tait! I couldn't believe it. She was our next door neighbour and she used to babysit us. She told me she had often visited Mrs Tait with her two sons. Suddenly I remembered the two 'posh' boys with their grey shorts who would come and play with us and Darkie, Mrs Tait's dog. Here was one son standing before me, Campbell McFarlane.

We arranged to meet at the Struther's Church in Glasgow, the next Saturday night. She and her son met me there. They prayed for Jesus to become Lord of their lives.

I was due to take an itinerant speaker, Barry Hawthorne, to Blairgowrie on the Monday and Campbell volunteered to drive us there as he was on holiday that week. He and Barry chatted the whole way. Campbell was full of questions which were duly answered. That evening on our return we went to Motherwell Business Men's Fellowship.

The speaker that night, John Edwards, covered all the questions Campbell had asked Barry on the way to Blairgowrie. "It's as if he was in the car with us!" stated Campbell. That's God for you!

That night Campbell responded to the gospel message again. On his way home he was baptised in the Spirit with the evidence of tongues. He was really moved. God moves in surprising ways, when you least expect it, even though you thought you were expecting God to move!

One verse I had prayed years ago was Romans 4:17 which says, "God... calls those things which do not exist as though they did".

Years before while I was on a mission in Rothesay, the pastor's wife, Liz, said I should pray and write down what I wanted in a husband. So I did. I kept the list in a notebook for years. Over the next weeks it was a voyage of discovery as literally one after another of the items on "My Husband" list became evident. Campbell was my list in human flesh!

I must admit I was shocked when he proposed. I didn't know what I expected but the question demanded a response.

Yes!

Because God had said to me we would be married in November, I wanted Campbell to choose the date.

"November." he said. "It has to November," as this was the only time he had free. So we arranged the wedding for November 1st 1997 in St Catherine's in Argyll near Strachur with our pastor, Bill Mercer taking the service jointly with Hugh Brown, a friend from Carnoustie.

Everything for the wedding was arranged very quickly and without any stress. About a month before my wedding, my sister in York asked if I could go and look after her two children while she was away on a course. The night before I was due to travel to York, my father's next door neighbour came over and told us that the new young couple across the road had been burgled. They had not been in their house for very long. Everyone felt sorry for them.

That night I went to bed but could not sleep as I had to get up and pray for the young couple. As I prayed I had a vision of the man leaning out of his upstairs window and waving to me from across the street. Then I saw his wife, whom I had not seen before, come out of their front door. She had long blond hair. I left it with the Lord after praying for their peace and safety and I went to sleep.

Next morning, just before I left, my Dad asked if I would do a quick favour and run down to the shop for milk. A simple request. Not a problem.

As I came out of the driveway to walk down the street, the man in the house across the street leaned out of his window and shouted to me across the road. It was exactly like in the vision I had seen.

"Hi I'm Jim. Are you Archie Dow's daughter?"

"Yes." I said. "Wait and I'll come down," he added.

So I waited. God's plans were about to unfold. We stood and chatted. He told me they had bought the house and were doing it up as it needed a lot of work. The front door opened and his wife joined us. She had long blond hair!

They invited me in.

God's timetable always supersedes ours. I went in to their living room and they told me all about the robbery, and all about the other unfortunate things they had experienced since moving in. As we chatted it was evident both were not saved. Her mother was a born again Christian who actually went to my friend's church. His best friend was a born again Baptist chap who had often talked to him about Jesus.

The wife gave her life to Jesus. As we prayed the Holy Spirit showed me there was a curse on the house which was broken as we prayed and they were both filled with peace.

Then it was milk and York, praising God all the way.

My sister returned on the Friday and we went down the street to find a pair of shoes for her daughter to wear with her flower girl's dress. The shoes were perfect and as we continued to walk down the street, we saw a wedding dress shop right where we stood. So we thought we would go in for a look. When we walked up the steep stairs and went through the door, we saw an absolutely beautiful outfit and I just knew it was the one! I tried it on and bought it with no stress whatsoever! We walked across the road to a hat shop and bought a hat which was a perfect match for the outfit. God knows I hate shopping and trying on clothes.

When I returned it was soon time for the wedding. We were married in St Catherine's and the reception took place in the Cobbler Hotel in Arrochar. It was a really happy occasion with family and friends. Comments were made about the peace everyone felt in the church.

A week's honeymoon in Israel followed. To see once more where Jesus lived and walked and spoke and prayed and healed and taught was awesome. There was another older honeymoon couple on the trip. We were privileged to share with them and pray for them and with them.

We returned to the house Campbell had bought previously in Paisley. As I was unpacking my last box of possessions, I prayed and said, "Lord when this box is unpacked what will I do? I give You my life afresh".

Half an hour later the phone rang. Campbell was a quantity surveyor working in a building contractor's yard in Glasgow a few days a week. His client asked if I would come and fill a gap answering the phone because he had just sacked his secretary. I started the next day. My new boss knew I was a Christian. I was told to answer the phones, take messages and pass them on to the right person and if it's quiet "just read your Bible or something."

The first day I worked in the office the air was blue! The cursing and swearing was prolific to say the least. That night I prayed and asked God to do something about their speech or lack of it! The next day, first thing in the morning, as the men gathered in the office to receive their jobs and orders for the day, the air was blue within seconds. The boss told them off for swearing in front of the new 'secretary'. I did not have to do a thing except pray.

Then he told me to get a jar or box or something, stick a label on it and charge the men 10p every time they swore. He informed them all the new regime would begin the next day so they had to come prepared to pay up or shut up! Within about three weeks the men had filled the large jar with their money which was then given to charity. However it was wonderful to see them come to a place where no more money was added. They had stopped swearing at work.

Working there was good. I mastered invoices, the computer and the Sage computer system for paying wages. Yet another learning curve.

The boss had a sore foot which annoyed and restricted him. We invited him to an FGB meeting in Glasgow where Allan Jones was speaking that night. Allan had a word of knowledge about a pain in someone's foot. "You told him!" the boss said to me, as if God does not know! He knew that I had not spoken to Allan so I explained about words of knowledge. The boss was informed that God knows everything and can reveal all kinds of information to His servants so He can help them. With encouragement and a supporting hand, the boss received prayer. The pain was gone. He tip-toed, jumped, stamped and there was no pain. He was amazed. He was healed!

At the building contractor's there were plenty of opportunities to share Jesus with the men, their girlfriends and wives. It was lovely to meet them and see the love of Jesus touch them. An unusual thing happened one day as I was asked to phone directory enquiries about obtaining a phone number. I was given the phone number and then the operator said, "I know this is highly irregular but may I ask you a question? Do you know what a Pentecostal church is?" His friend had recently gone to one in Edinburgh and he was not at all sure about it!

How amazing is our Father in heaven to work outside the normal box and answer someone's question!

During my time at the contractor's office, I learned something of which I had previously been ignorant, all because I had to drop off a worksheet to the work's foreman at a local pub because he needed it right away. Pubs were not places I had frequented, however, on this occasion I saw something that showed me the fascination pubs had for people.

Their local was like a home from home for men and women to enjoy their friendships. Their banter and the sharing of problems and woes were very evident. They enjoyed the personal aspects of pub life not just the drinks and enjoyed a good laugh with their mates! It was like an extra dimension of family life. The only snag was many did not want to live in their actual family role, being a good husband and father. The characters I met were so very nice, quick witted, fly, sarcastic and very helpful. Pubs were places where relationships were forged and good camaraderie experienced. However a burning question arose, how do we reach the people God loves in pubs? Go in!

During this time we used to have house meetings with many itinerant speakers. Many stayed overnight and Campbell loved giving them breakfast next morning asking them all his questions. "How old was Adam when God made him?"

The boss even had one speaker come to do a house meeting at his home. This Christian stuff was all new to him!

I had been there in the office for nearly a year when I was praying one night, I heard, "Tell the boss you'll leave at Christmas. He has five weeks to find a new secretary; I have a new job for you". The boss wasn't happy but got someone a thousand times better.

I was praying one day before Christmas about the new job God said He had for me when the phone rang. It was Mr Brown, my old headmaster from Clarkston Primary in Airdrie. He had heard I was back in the area and offered me a job. I had to re-register with the General Teaching Council and Educational Institute of Scotland before starting the teaching job back in the school I left all those years ago. I began my new job back in teaching on January 7th 1998 just like that! I remembered a prophetic word from years ago that I would one day be back in the classroom.

Truly God knows the plans He has to prosper us and not to harm us, plans to give us a future and a hope.(Jeremiah 29:11)

Leaving the house at seven in the morning, I travelled to Clarkston Primary in Airdrie for five years working in that brilliant school. I had marvellous opportunities with staff, cleaners, and parents. Curses were broken off, enabling one teacher not to miscarry;

people were healed, saved and delivered. God even found the right home for someone.

I met one child who was suffering from severe depression and family trauma. The Holy Spirit had me phone and ask the parent if I could pray for her child. She said that would be good but could I come to their home which was all highly irregular! While there, she told me the whole story because she knew the root of her child's behaviour. The parents had tried their best but God did the rest! Both the child and the parents were touched. Prayer changes things and if you do not believe it, try praying.

God had me leave Clarkston and take a job share job for three months in a different school where I was job sharing with a Christian teacher. The class was lovely but there was one disturbed and needy pupil, evident by their disruptive behaviour, who was causing us great concern. We used to phone each other giving an update on class events. So we prayed for this child and over the weeks we saw the child respond.

Towards the end on my third month, I was informed that the child psychologist would be visiting the class to observe this particular child. All I had to do was teach as normal and let him observe from the back of the class. The afternoon ended, the children left then he came to discuss the child with me. The first question he asked was, "Is this the same child?" What had happened to cause the changes? This child was definitely not the child he had been working with! I simply stated what the job share teacher and I had done in praying daily for the child. The power of prayer and the fact that God answers prayer was shared with him. I told him what we specifically had prayed for and how we had prayed in the name of Jesus and the power of the blood of Jesus. He sat silently, listening, taking notes. I had boldness and said that he had just evidenced the power of prayer working to bring about such incredible change. Then he said his wife believed the same as us. God moves us anywhere He likes. The world is His mission field.

When this job ended it was back to Clarkston Primary. Every year I was given a new stage of class so it was new work to prepare and plan all the time. Talk about a challenge!

Life was busy with work and more work. Although I was married I felt alone. I had no friends in Paisley except the ladies from Aglow. Each month speakers came to the Aglow meetings and it was beautiful the way God spoke a 'now' word each month into my life. It was also a nice night out with a lovely meal in the local Watermill Hotel where I enjoyed chatting to the ladies and hearing about what God was doing in their lives.

Then once again five years later, Christmas was soon approaching and in prayer I felt to stop teaching at Clarkston Primary. It did not make sense to Campbell to leave a great job I loved, especially when I had no new job to go to yet again!

Many times what God does and says, does not make sense. He just asks for our obedience. So I handed in my notice yet again. Friends and family thought I was mad but I knew what God had said, so I did what He asked me. Following Jesus is never boring! It can be exciting and nerve racking at the same time!

On the last day of school before Christmas in North Lanarkshire, I had intended visiting my father and sister that afternoon as they lived a few miles away from the school. Their presents were in the car boot and as the school finished at 1.30pm I would have plenty time to visit them before going home.

When I got into the car, however, I heard, "Go home right now!" It was very clear. So a change of plan meant I went straight home to Paisley. Coming into the house and taking off my coat, I heard Campbell call from the upstairs office, "There's someone on the phone for you!"

It was Renfrewshire Council asking if I was free to work in Mary Russell School in Paisley. Could I go on Monday to see the school as they stopped at 3pm on Monday just before Christmas? I had had my name on the Council's teaching list for five years without one single call. Now, however, it was God's timing to open this door on my own door step.

When I visited the school the sense of peace was beautiful and I recognised God's hand in it all. The blessing of God was amazing. I started in the January of 2003 in the special needs school, which was another huge learning curve. At college I had only done one placement in an autistic unit one afternoon each month for six months. This job was getting out of the boat again!

I had prayed for me to have a friend in Paisley. Unbeknown to me, my soon to be friend had prayed for a friend just like her. She taught in the class across the corridor from me and was invaluable as she helped me settle in. She had been there for years and knew the routine and the children. I needed to pray and ask God to help me work with these children because, once again, I was way out of my depth. I was initially put in a Primary 6 class till the teacher returned from her maternity leave.

I invited my new colleague to come to a woman's meeting in Irvine at which I was speaking. She came, got saved and baptised in the Spirit. Next morning she heard the Holy Spirit whisper to her, "Be careful to obey

Me in everything." My new friend was now my sister in Christ!

Within weeks the pupils and staff were asking if we were sisters! We were so alike! I had asked for a friend. She had asked for a friend just like her. God matched us up.

When the teacher came back after her maternity leave, I figured it would be a move to another school somewhere else. However, they wanted to keep me on, so I was given primary and secondary classes for the month before the summer holidays and then was surprised when they offered me a new post in the school after the holidays as an ICT teacher. I barely knew how to turn on a computer never mind teach basic skills. However, I did a lot of work over the seven weeks holiday and mastered basic skills, just!

I used to say in PWAMM, I was a 'FAT' person. By that I meant I was Flexible, Adaptable, and a Team player. That has stood me in good stead over the years in every job I have had. If I believe God is truly in control of every area of my life then if He permitted something I would go with Him and try not to work against Him. The old lesson of having two choices affects every area of our lives and we can respond or react; the choice is always ours; the choice is always mine! One helps the situation, the other aggravates it. I may have felt out my depth yet again, but with God all things are possible, especially walking on water!

While teaching in the special needs school, God made a way for me to travel to Turin in Italy along with two friends. There was a Bible school being held and an invitation was given for Barbara Smith to speak there and my friend Joyce and I went to support and pray for her. I had asked for unpaid leave to allow me to go as it was during term time and I was given permission. The favour of God works all the time!

The Turin Bible School went well. Many were touched mightily by the power of God, in words of prophecy and healing and deliverance. After lunch one day, I was suddenly asked to speak after the praise finished. God filled my mouth and I spoke about my personal experience of abuse. An African woman cried all the time I spoke and there were others who also wept. She was set free and healed.

The ministry time lasted for ages as people received healing from sexual abuse. One pastor, who had travelled hours to attend the Bible School, suddenly took my arm and that of the interpreter and shoved a mobile phone in my hand and asked me to pray for his wife back home as she also had been abused and had had no ministry and needed help. God's Word says in 2 Corinthians 1:3-5 "Blessed be the God and Father of our Lord Jesus Christ, the Father of mercies and God of all comfort, who comforts us in all our tribulation, that we may be able to comfort those who are in any trouble, with the comfort with which we ourselves are comforted by God. For as the sufferings of Christ abound in us, so our consolation also abounds through Christ".

I had never experienced that challenge before and as always had to lean on the Holy Spirit's help. As ever all I can do is ask God to fill my mouth with His words and pray with love and compassion for the person, believing that because it worked for me, it will work for others also.

At a break, the pastor in charge of the Bible School asked me to go with him to speak to someone. An Italian businessman wanted to share his heart with us, with the pastor translating. He had told no other living soul. It was heart wrenching to listen to how both his father and uncle, for years, repeatedly raped him as a young child. It was even sadder to hear how, although he was happily married and had children, there was something driving him to seek out homosexual liaisons. People fail to understand that when there is an open door through abuse, demons come in and cause a weakness in that area. He repented and was set free. An email came a year later to say that the man had had no more sinful liaisons and that he was free indeed.

I loved my time in the Turin school. There were many opportunities to share Jesus, pray for people and see God move in their situations. I felt privileged to accompany Barbara. I went to Turin often on God's assignment.

On my return from Turin, I felt God telling me to hold a house meeting in a friend's house and invite the staff who were recently saved and filled with the Spirit. God gave me specific speakers to ask. God is amazing as He spoke prophetically into the teachers' lives and circumstances and they could not believe how accurate the words were. It was so different from their usual church services. Now they realised that truly God knew them individually. It was another lesson in religion versus the Spirit. The Holy Spirit is real and He moves and speaks as we give Him space and freedom to do so.

God's connections are everywhere if we appreciate and recognise them. I was asked to pray for a lady who stayed not too far from my father's house and God set her free. She knew the touch of God on her life and said she had some friends who also needed God's touch, so a house meeting was arranged in her area. As there were so many people who needed a touch from God, we hired a bigger venue where special, anointed speakers 'just so happened to be passing through'. We had one meeting a month with them in both Paisley and North Lanarkshire which kept my new friend and I busy. Many were saved, healed, delivered and filled with the Holy Spirit. Many lives were changed and God got all the glory.

Campbell and I would go away to weekend conferences held in a variety of places. The teaching was always excellent and the power of the Holy Spirit moved mightily. We were extremely blessed.

The little fellowship in Argyll we went to was amazing. It may have seemed out of the way but God was present and moving. Over the years many people came to the Sunday services and the conferences we had every New Year. It was brilliant to see the many wonderful ways God moved. Many drug addicts were saved, bodies healed, minds renewed and lives transformed by the power of His Word and Spirit. The pastor Bill and Maisie his wife demonstrated how to live selfless lives.

In our daily lives we met many people to invite to the church. A woman came one Sunday and the pastor started to speak about spiritualism instead of what he had prepared. We thought he had got it wrong! Guess who was really into spiritualism? The lady was taught from the Word of God and repented and was saved. How we need to be led by the Spirit and go with the flow even it does seem way off track!

There was another lady who came from the local area who said things bluntly to everyone whether they asked for it or not. She came up to me one Sunday morning and suddenly said, "I don't like you!" and walked away. What was it God says about loving your neighbour? I racked my brain to see if I had offended her. I could not come up with one thing. After the service she told me exactly why she did not like me. I understood it!

It was very simple really but it was a necessary eye-opener to me at the time. After the service I often had people to see but would just say 'hello' to others in passing on my way to whoever I was to do business with. She was quite right as I was unaware of her feelings of being ignored. Did I show her I cared about her? No! My actions showed her she was unloved, passed quickly over and many a time not even noticed! What would Jesus do?

It is so easy to get wrapped up in our own agendas that we do not even notice the people who are part of the Body of Christ alongside us! It was a timely rebuke from the Lord. However, the damage was done as far as she was concerned and she did not recover from my rejection of her!

Campbell had not been feeling well for a long time. In fact the first day we had a date, as we cycled around Millport, he apologised for not feeling well. He said he had had tests as he had been having stomach pains for quite a while. All the initial tests showed nothing sinister. This was what he was told for six years.

He would come home from work, have tea and go to bed. There were times he would be writhing on the bed in dreadful agony. He suffered from terrible bouts of profuse sweating. The bed needed changing sometimes more than once a night, every night for weeks at a time. Terrible itching drove him mad at all hours of the day and night. I have to say it drove me mad too! The only relief he got was by taking a metal brush to scratch his skin! Many visits and tests later and, they still could not see anything wrong.

Added to his health situation and the continual pain, the pressure of work escalated as deadlines loomed near. He had his own business and worked exceptionally diligently.

Finally they diagnosed his problems. He had a stent put in one kidney as it was not functioning properly. He had a tumour on his spine which ate his vertebrae away, thereby exposing the nerves in his spinal column.

Finally they reached a diagnosis from the recent tests undertaken; 'retroperitoneal fibrosis and cancer.' That word strikes fear in hearts and minds; with all sorts of tormenting thoughts that rob people of peace. Chemotherapy and radiotherapy followed and life was stormy to say the least.

We experienced a very shaky time in our marriage which resulted in us being separated for periods of time. The first was only for five weeks, and then we were reconciled. The second was for eight months before we were again reconciled.

Over several months we had considered buying a house possibly in Irvine, Largs or Beith. While praying about moving I saw Stirling Castle and the surrounding area but Campbell always said no to moving up north!

However, in 2007 we moved to Alloa and were settled into a new house. We saw an advert in a local paper for a prophetic meeting which an Assemblies of

God church was holding in Stirling. We both went on the Saturday to the meetings which were very good. We discovered that one of the speakers was speaking at the AOG church in Stirling the next morning. I love it when a plan of God comes together. The speaker spoke on the very Scripture God gave me when we moved to the area about two months previously which was Isaiah 42:16, "I will bring the blind by a way they did not know; I will lead them in paths they have not known. I will make darkness light before them, and crooked places straight. These things I will do for them, and not forsake them".

God had shown me the church to go to. It was a great wee church with terrific pastors, Ron and Kerry Edwards, and their lovely family. It felt like home so quickly and I loved it and them.

We had super teaching, great praise and worship, good fellowship and we also enjoyed the special speakers God brought there too. The pastor's wife and I would do 'street work' on a Saturday whenever we could, usually near Stirling Cross. We shared the gospel, prayed for people's healing or their problems. We need more Jesus on the streets all over Scotland.

I was on the Stirlingshire teaching supply list and was kept busy in schools for months at a time.

However things at home became very sad and bad in our relationship. God gave me a love for my husband like I could not believe. It did not matter what he did or said or how his words hurt or caused pain. I loved him. God was very gracious because He protected me. I went to a meeting one day and someone gave me a picture of God giving me knight's armour to wear. I soon found out why! A few years later, the picture was of this armour being taken off me and me then being placed in an army tank. God was showing me the severity of what was to come.

Medication made Campbell suffer from paranoia and he believed all kinds of untruths and would not choose to believe the truth. As a result both of us found communication hard and when that goes it leads down a slippery slope. We had gone to a weekend in Gartmore House where Val Kincaid was speaking. She prophesied over us that God would turn the chaos in our home to order. A promise I stood on till God did it.

I kept praying for God's guidance during many difficult months where suspicion and lack of trust abounded. The final straw came on Sunday evening 20th December 2009 when the pressure was too much and Campbell snapped and I was told to get out. Not a pleasant experience I know, but I knew God was doing something and so I accepted the situation, but I would have to find somewhere else to stay.

The next day was Monday and I was not teaching, so I got up and prayed, "Lead me God!" We were still living in Alloa at that time and I went down the street and parked in the car park and walked onto the street where I had a choice to either go to the left or the right or walk straight ahead.

As I looked to my right I caught sight of a metal sign sticking out of the wall saying 'Impact'. Now I have to say I had seen the word IMPACT on brochures, in shops, in a hotel, and had read the word in books and papers. I could not escape the word 'impact' which I had seen regularly for three months prior to this. I told my friend I did not understand fully what it meant, but I knew the word was significant somehow. I had never seen the sign there on the wall before. It was an estate agent and the sign was only displayed for a few days and was then taken down. God had given a personal signpost to guide me.

When I went in to the estate agent's office he said he had no flats to rent until five minutes before I had arrived. He had just received a call from a woman who had tried for two years to sell her flat but was now telling him to rent it out. The owner was a minister who bought the flat and then got a new job elsewhere. God had kept that flat for two years just for me. It was bright, light and spacious; God knows what I like. I rented the flat initially for six months not knowing I would be there for three years.

I got the keys on the 23rd and moved in before Christmas. The estate agent said he had never seen anyone move in as quickly as the process normally takes two weeks or longer. But God! I was settled very quickly. I watched once again as everything fell into place. Once more, the favour of God took my breath away.

Not knowing how things were with Campbell was the hardest part. Campbell did ask me for three weeks to go back but it was not permitted by God. For sanity's sake, I kept focused on God and served Him. Worry has never changed one thing regarding the situations I have been in; however, prayer has changed everything all the time. If I trust God with my life, I can also trust God with my husband's life.

I knew the Alloa house was up for sale for nearly three years, despite the price being reduced, with only one viewer. When praying one day, I felt God say, "Be very still and fast and pray in tongues from 6.00am till 9.00pm for the first Thursday and from 9.00am to 6.00pm the second Thursday." This was possible as I did not work on a Thursday at the time.

On the second Thursday I had an appointment to pray with people after their work. At 9.00pm they were on the point of leaving when Campbell phoned to say the house was sold and he was moving back to Paisley. God knows why we need to obey and pray as sometimes prayer and fasting is the only thing that shifts situations or brings a breakthrough.

So Campbell went back to Paisley so he could be near the hospital as he needed more treatment.

While in the Assemblies of God church in Stirling, I was told to use the name that was on my birth certificate. It is fascinating the way God makes His will clear. Abraham has always played an important part in my life. Specific verses have been used to guide me at various times and in various ways. This time as I read the Bible what jumped out at me was the name change.

Abram which meant 'high father' was changed to Abraham 'father of a multitude' (Genesis 17:5). His wife Sarai 'my princess' was changed to Sarah - 'mother of nations.' Every time I read about Mary my heart would silently say "That's my real name. The one on my birth certificate and the name I use in my signature." Once again I prayed and asked God to confirm His word. Weeks passed and I received a book in the post in a brown envelope which was torn when I received it and there was no covering letter. There was also a huge dirty footprint over the front of the envelope. The book was about a woman's testimony of how God changed her name from Jenny to Jennifer and her testimony was very similar to mine.

Just after that, I went to a meeting in Kilsyth where there was a special speaker that night called Graham Unsworth. At the ministry time I asked for prayer. I simply said, "As the Spirit leads". I gave him no name and although I was nameless to him I was known to God who knows everything all the time. The speaker prayed in the Spirit then prayed accurately into my situation regarding Campbell from whom I was still estranged. It was almost as if he lived with us and was familiar with every area of our lives.

He kept saying "Lord you know Mary... Mary... Mary..."

At the end, my friend who was standing beside me said to him, "You nearly got that right. Her name is May not Mary." He looked straight at her and said, "My dear, I got it right. Her name is Mary and the Lord wants her to use her real name!"

Amazing!

The last thing that confirmed my name was going to change, took place in an African church in Edinburgh. In the middle of her talk, the speaker pointed to me and said, "Her name shall be called Mary". She did not remember saying it.

Now I was willing to use my real name Mary but how exactly do you do that seeing as how I have always been known as May? It was simple really. After church the next Sunday, Ron the pastor, explained to everyone that God had told me to use my real name of

Mary and from that time on I was Mary! I understand not everyone finds it easy to call me Mary when they have known me for years as May but I appreciate everyone's support.

Why does God change names? God is free to do what He wants and has His reasons. I believe like the Bible shows, it's a change of role or mission or purpose. One thing I have definitely noticed about my name change is I choose to be like Mary to sit at the feet of Jesus and not rush around and be busy all the time like I used to be.

I had been in the 'IMPACT' flat in Tullibody for three years, and one day I visited my friend in Paisley and was stuck in traffic for fifteen minutes because of road works on Glasgow Road on the way to her house. I sat thanking God for Stirlingshire. The beauty of the area and the quiet roads compared to the busyness of Paisley was a blessing to me. Suddenly I heard, "Get used to this. You're coming back to Paisley."

I went to see my friend and told her what had just happened. "Oh that's good." she said. "Last week after I was on the phone to you, I put the phone down, turned round and out of my mouth I heard myself say, "She's coming back to Paisley!"

Well I loved living in the flat in Tullibody where I had friends and strangers to stay all the time. I had made good friends. I was going to an alive church, felt loved and was supported. I loved the people, thoroughly enjoyed the scenery, the church and everything about life there. To be honest I was not overjoyed at the thought of moving back to Paisley! Anyway where in Paisley and how would I get there? So I prayed for confirmation.

My friend and I went to a weekend conference in Rothesay. At the end of the service on the Sunday, we were to form groups of four and pray for each other. When the group prayed for me, Linda, a friend from Perth, had a picture of me standing on a veranda of a flat wearing a beautiful Paisley patterned scarf. I had not told her what God had said about me returning to Paisley.

"Does that make sense to you?" she asked. Yes! It was confirmation. God sure does know how to get the message across to us loud and clear so that there is no room for doubt or error! It would appear I would be going to Paisley right enough. So it is over to you Lord!

Just after this, my former pastor, Bill, from St Catherine's was having one of his monthly meetings in the Ramada Hotel near Glasgow Airport. I used to take some friends each month for the Saturday night and Sunday morning meeting where we would stay in the rooms at a special rate.

During the service I had a picture of me standing knocking on a light coloured door. I knew in my heart that it was where Campbell was and got this sense of, "Go and see Campbell." I told my friend, Pat, and she prayed that, if God was in this, I would hear Campbell's name being mentioned before I left the hotel. We all had lunch and after this I went outside to say goodbye to my friends, Matt and Pat, from the Borders. So far I had not heard Campbell's name, so assumed I had got it wrong. I went back into the hotel and collected my overnight bag. While I was saying my goodbyes to everyone, Jim Barr, who had turned up unexpectedly to our morning service, indicated that he wanted to speak to me as he had not seen me for quite a long time, so I put down my bags. He told me he had seen someone I knew who was asking him if he had seen me! Campbell!

He had met Campbell at the Royal Alexandra Hospital at one of his appointments. He detected a change in Campbell and told me he believed that God had touched him and softened his heart. Well, now I knew I had to go and see Campbell who had already told me where he had moved to in Paisley. Just to make sure I would be obedient and go, a lady asked me for a lift which was on the way to Campbell's flat.

When I arrived my heart was filled with an incredible peace. The door was just like in the vision I had had that morning so I knocked and waited. Campbell opened the door and the words he uttered right away were, "Thank you Lord for answering my prayers. But your timing is lousy as of all days I am due to go out in about half an hour". It was time enough for God.

Phone calls and catching up over the next weeks enabled me to see that there was no doubt he had changed. Over the next months God made it plain that it was time to be properly reconciled. So I gave up my flat in Tullibody and I moved into Campbell's second floor flat in Paisley in obedience to the will of God for my life. Once again I settled in very quickly. It was as if we had never been separated and we enjoyed peace, harmony, love and joy and order instead of chaos just as God had prophesied.

For the first few months I had no specific leading as to which church to go to, so each Sunday I would visit different churches looking for a place to belong. I had gone round the churches once when I prayed, "Lord where will I go today?" "Go to Elim." I was told.

So I did. I also went the next week. At the ministry time at the end of the service of that second week, the pastor said that he wanted the young folk to pray for the adults. One young boy, Nana, came up and prayed for me. The first words he said were, "Lord you know you have brought Mary here for a purpose." God had confirmed His will once again. I quickly settled into the body of believers in Elim.

Campbell's health was deteriorating and he needed another operation and more radiotherapy. He got over that hurdle.

My name was added to the Renfrewshire teaching supply list and I was kept busy with work in local schools. I enjoyed my time in all of them as the staff were very welcoming and helpful. It was like moving from mission field to mission field.

In September 2014 Campbell woke up one morning and found he had difficulty standing up straight. Something had happened to him. We were due to visit the palliative care doctor at the hospice that afternoon. He took one look at Campbell and had him admitted to hospital. Tests and X-rays showed his spine was unstable due to the pressure from the tumour and that his spine could possibly break if something was not done to prevent this. He spent two weeks in Royal Alexandra Hospital in Paisley and a further two weeks in the Southern General hospital in Glasgow. The surgeon there inserted titanium rods and screws into his spine to stop it from breaking. The operation went well but not the pain control. He suffered horrific pain before they managed to get it under control. He was very brave and did not complain.

During this time I was really tired preparing work for school, teaching and visiting Campbell every day. He suggested that I give up teaching. I prayed and decided to have a chat with the headmistress who actually was coming to tell me that my job was ending as those specific funds had run out. God knows the perfect time for release. I felt led to enquire about retiring as I was sixty on 6th of September. As I had taught for nearly 25 years I was eligible for retirement and stopped teaching as Campbell needed help and care.

In 2015 my friend, Barbara, invited me to a Bible Holiday in Ischia in Italy. Campbell suggested I should go but there was a problem as he could not be left on his own. However, a friend who was a carer was free to come for the week to look after him.

So I went in a party of thirteen women from Scotland to Ischia in Italy. We stayed in a family run hotel called 'Terme la Pergola which had thermal pools. There was a time of praise and worship each night. For three days of the seven we were there, we had a conference with a meeting every afternoon and evening. It was a wonderful time of fellowship and teaching. The teaching was about Birthing, Vision and Esther.

God spoke powerfully to me about His vision for the next season of my life. On the last night one of the women from Turin asked to speak to me. She shared her story of how her life had been impacted by what I had shared in Turin in 2006. She had had a dream where she saw a two year old baby being raped. When she looked at this baby, it looked like her and when she woke up she prayed and asked the Lord, "Who is this baby?" God said that she was the baby. Her parents thought she would have forgotten being raped by her cousin when she was two and they told her they did not know what to do about this.

She left Kenya and came to Turin and stayed in a house with some other girls and a man. This man raped her even though she dressed well and did not entice him in any way. Another time she escaped from being raped. She felt shamed. She was told she would need to go to the police as a new law had been passed that stated rapists would be jailed for five years. She received no support, went to court and he was freed. She feared for her life because his family and friends had threatened her.

She came to the Bible school in Turin in 2006 where I had shared my testimony. She responded to the prayer for all the abuse in her life and she was delivered and healed and the Lord set her wonderfully free. The abuse stopped. She always believed that God had a specific job for her to do and a few years later she got a job in a rape crisis centre where she has been used to help many women in similar situations seeing them set free also. Many of the women she helps are Muslims and they see such a difference in her life compared to theirs.

Because they ask her lots of questions she has an open door to share her testimony of what God has done for her. She sees women get saved and begin a new life. We met one of them when she came with her to Ischia.

The Word of God will always accomplish what it is sent to do; it may be instant or it may take time but it does what He sends it to do for His glory.(Isaiah 55:11)

It was Campbell's desire to have a dog as he has always been dog daft. We got a beautiful miniature dachshund called Lilly. Talk about a joy! She made us laugh so much with her antics.

About six years ago God gave me a word about taking me to where the bluebells grow. In God's time He knows everything. It was decided that we should look for a new house with a garden for Lilly. After much praying we bought a new home in Elderslie. Before we moved in, however, we were told that Campbell had lung cancer. After thirty six doses of radiotherapy we finally moved at the end of November 2016 and discovered that Bluebell Woods was at the end of our street! We settled in really happily to our new home.

On 15th of February we were told the cancer had spread to Campbell's liver and there was nothing more they could do. He had possibly days or weeks to live. He hoped he would see the middle of April to give him time to put his affairs in order.

Over the years my husband had prayed about twenty one times asking Jesus to come into his life, yet he had absolutely no assurance of salvation. He found it difficult to believe God loved him. You see Campbell did not love himself.

He struggled to grasp the fact that God could forgive his poor choices, bad behaviour, angry episodes and violent outbursts.

To Campbell, it seemed too simple that when we asked God to forgive us and we repented of our sin we were forgiven! It seemed too easy and we got off too lightly.

The missing truth was Jesus paid the price for all our sins to be forgiven. He took the punishment we were due when he died in our place. Campbell's intellect could not grasp the simplicity of truth therefore he could not accept what the Bible said about forgiveness or the love of God. A relationship with Jesus was impossible for him to enjoy because of his wrong thinking. He was worried about facing death because he did not have the certainty he would be accepted into heaven.

About five weeks before he died, he asked to speak to Tom my pastor. When I came back from walking Lilly, I instantly knew that Campbell had finally made his peace with God. All fear of death had gone. He had finally met Jesus as Lord and Saviour and had given his life to Him, believing the truth of God's word. He knew he was heaven bound. No more panic. No more doubt. He knew God could be trusted. Truth had touched his heart and changed him. God had given him assurance of eternal life.

Campbell encountered Jesus in a most beautiful way and went to heaven very peacefully on 12th April 2017. Our time together was special and although sad, we knew, and I know, the reality of heaven as his eternal home. I will see him again. I know that as fact.

Looking back at my life I see it as God said it would be. Years ago while I was in Stirling, the pastor's wife had a picture of my life. Kerry said my life was like an orange. At the time I did not really appreciate what God meant by that. However, I now recognise that when I look at my life, I see it as segments of events, times, seasons, dealings, trials, but most of all, adventures.

There is really nothing special about my life except for the difference Jesus has made to it. I can honestly say I have enjoyed the journey with all of the ups and downs I have experienced along the way. Looking back, I am so glad I said "yes" to Jesus all those years ago. Life with Jesus is really an awesome adventure and a privilege for anyone. It does not matter what a person's age or nationality happens to be. All that is required is giving Jesus the reins of our life and allowing Him lead us where we need to be, for the purpose of doing what He wants us to do.

I would like to encourage everyone to share their stories and tell many people about the difference Jesus really makes. After all, Jesus is the same yesterday, today and forever and because this is true, let's enjoy being available to Him so He can speak through us. We will see people saved, healed, set free and following Him as Lord, Saviour and Friend!

I look forward to experiencing the next segments of my life, as I keep walking step by step in obedience to His will. I know I will experience the segments God already has waiting and prepared just for me; they are to be tasted and enjoyed and I can't wait!

Printed in Poland
by Amazon Fulfillment
Poland Sp. z o.o., Wrocław